LOGICAL DATA MODELING

INTEGRATED SERIES IN INFORMATION SYSTEMS

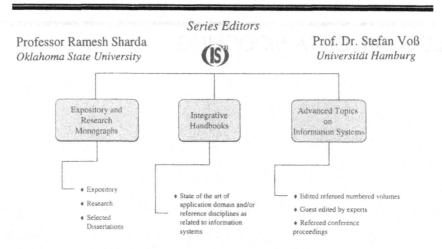

Series Editors

Professor Ramesh Sharda
Oklahoma State University

Prof. Dr. Stefan Voß
Universität Hamburg

Other published titles in the series:

E-BUSINESS MANAGEMENT: *Integration of Web Technologies with Business Models/* Michael J. Shaw

VIRTUAL CORPORATE UNIVERSITIES: *A Matrix of Knowledge and Learning for the New Digital Dawn/* Walter R.J. Baets & Gert Van der Linden

SCALABLE ENTERPRISE SYSTEMS: *An Introduction to Recent Advances/* edited by Vittal Prabhu, Soundar Kumara, Manjunath Kamath

LEGAL PROGRAMMING: *Legal Compliance for RFID and Software Agent Ecosystems in Retail Processes and Beyond/* Brian Subirana and Malcolm Bain

LOGICAL DATA MODELING
What it is and How to do it

Alan Chmura
Eastern New Mexico University, Portales, New Mexico

J. Mark Heumann
META Group EMEA, Dubai, UAE

 Springer

Alan Chmura
Eastern New Mexico University
Portales, New Mexico

J. Mark Heumann
META Group EMEA
Dubai, UAE

ISBN 978-1-4419-1989-2

e-ISBN 978-0-387-22962-1   Printed on acid-free paper.

9 8 7 6 5 4 3 2 1

springeronline.com

Contents

Preface

This book is directed toward three groups of people:

- Business subject matter experts
- Information technology professionals
- Advanced students in Computer Science, Management Information Systems, and e-Business.

The book's purpose is to teach the basics of logical data modeling—specifically, data modeling for relational database management systems—in simple, practical terms and in a business context. We feel that relational data modeling is better than object oriented data modeling, hierarchical data modeling, and network data modeling when it comes to modeling real business activities.

We have written this book from the point of view of the project leader or project manager, a subject matter expert charged with developing a relational database and the information systems which interact with that database. Of course, real-world data modeling is best done by experienced data modelers. But by reading and understanding this book, the enterprise-side project manager should gain enough understanding of data modeling to follow what is going on and help communicate that understanding to the people who know the business, do the work, and are going to be affected by the system being built.

The person who masters this material should be able to

- show an understanding of the business function of logical data modeling

- show an understanding of the role of collaboration and community in building a data model
- collect business rules for a functional area
- write formal Business Statements
- translate those Business Statements into logical data model entities, attributes, and associations
- build a data map
- create an entity list
- validate the data model against normalization and other standards
- assist a Database Administrator in translating the logical data model into a physical data model.

Advisory

The Boy Scouts place this statement at the beginning of every recipe they publish:

Read instructions twice before starting.

Sounds like good advice to us.

A NOTE ON TERMINOLOGY

There is no universal agreement regarding the terms used in logical data modeling. The following table shows many essential terms used in this book and corresponding terms in several data modeling notations other than ours. The table is not intended to exhaust the vocabulary of data modeling, nor are all data modeling notations represented. We do not claim that the terms we have provided are necessarily the best or the only terms, or that we have completed work on the matrix.

We have excluded several flavors of entity (Principal, Role, Structure, and Type) because we have discovered few if any directly correlating examples in notations other than Information Engineering. Strong and weak entity flavors, used in some notations, do not correspond directly with Information Engineering notation.

Unified Modeling Language (UML) is a generalized language. It deals with objects and classes (constructs within the object-oriented paradigm), not data *per se*, and it is usually used for defining the components of software applications other than relational databases (the kind of database for which we are modeling). Because UML is generalized and object-oriented, its terminology maps only approximately to the terminology used in this book.

The following sources were used in preparing this table:

- Chen Entity Relationship: Chen 1976.
- IDEF1X: US Government 1993.
- Oracle/Barker: Halpin 2000; Barker 1990; Burek 2004.
- Semantic Object Model: Kroenke 2002.
- UML: Object Management Group 2003.

This book	Chen Entity-Relationship	IDEF1X	Oracle/Barker	Semantic Object Model	UML
association	relationship	relationship	relationship	semantic object attribute, object link	association
attribute	attribute	attribute	attribute	attribute, property	attribute
cardinality	cardinality, connectivity	cardinality	cardinality, degree	cardinality	cardinality, multiplicity
categorizing association	---	categorizing relationship	---	---	---
child	weak entity, dependent entity	child entity	---	subtype object	child
compound primary key	---	composite key	---	group identifier	---
data map	---	diagram	---	semantic object model	class diagram
entity	entity, entity type, entity set	entity	entity type, entity	class	class
foreign key	---	foreign key, migrated attribute	---	---	---
instance	entity	entity instance	---	object instance	instance
identifying association	---	identifying relationship	---	---	---
intersecting entity	intersection entity, bridge entity	associative entity	---	association object	association class
key	identifier	key	unique identifier	---	---
mandatory	---	mandatory	mandatory	mandatory	---
non-identifying association	---	non-identifying relationship	---	---	---

This book	Chen Entity-Relationship	IDEF1X	Oracle/ Barker	Semantic Object Model	UML
non-key attribute	descriptor	non-key attribute	---	---	---
optional	optional	optional	optional	optional	---
optionality	optionality, existence	---	optionality	---	---
parent	entity, independent entity	parent entity	---	parent object	parent, superclass
primary key	entity type identifier	primary key	primary identifier, primary key	object identifier	---
recursive entity	unary	---	recursive	---	---
secondary entity	---	categorizing entity	---	---	child, subclass
subtype	sub-type, entity subtype	sub-type, sub-class, entity category	subtype	subtype object	subtype, generalization
supertype	super-type	generic entity, super-type, super-class	supertype	parent object	supertype

Acknowledgments

We acknowledge with gratitude the contributions made by Clive Finkelstein, the Father of Information Engineering. His books

- *An Introduction to Information Engineering: From Strategic Planning to Information Systems* (Sydney: Addison-Wesley, 1990) and
- *Information Engineering: Strategic Systems Development* (Sydney: Addison-Wesley, 1992)

have been of inestimable value.

We wish also to thank

- Visible Systems Corporation for their support, both for giving us use of their enterprise modeling tool Visible Advantage and for answering the many questions that arose in the course of writing
- Craig Mullins, *Database Administration: The Complete Guide to Practices and Procedures* (Boston: Addison-Wesley, 2002), for his contribution to our discussion of denormalization (Chapter 12)
- Michael C. Reingruber and William W. Gregory, *The Data Modeling Handbook* (New York: Wiley, 1994), for their contributions to our discussion of attributes (Chapter 7), verification (Chapter 9), and normalization (Chapter 10).
- Peter Rob and Elie Semaan, *Databases: Design, Development, and Deployment Using Microsoft Access*, 2nd ed. (New York: Irwin McGraw-Hill, 2004), for their contribution to our discussion of normalization (Chapter 10).

Chapter 1

GETTING STARTED

Where in we see how disorganized the company really is

It's been a good day, your first day as the new Production Manager of Pinebeach Screen Printing and Embroidery. At least, it was a good day until the owner dropped in.

"Hey, do you know anybody that can build a database?" he says. "Basically, we need something to retrieve our customer information and document the work orders."

Work orders. The words make you shudder. The paper-based work order system is a nightmare, and all the customer information is on note cards.

"It takes Stephanie three to five hours a day to compile orders," the boss continues. "And we're growing. With our growth, we need to look at the big picture. We need to see exactly what we have, what is pending, and what's completed. We can't do that with our current paper-based system.

"We're doing a lot of unnecessary work every day. I don't know all the parameters, but the system has to be user friendly. Many of our work order processes aren't written down. If my wife and I were to die tomorrow, you would have to take over, and you wouldn't know half of what we do."

Whoa. You hadn't thought of that. But he's right.

The boss continues. It's like he's thinking out loud. "We need to free up time to generate more revenue. We need to have a computer to go to so we don't lose work orders. We can't just shut down the paper and pencil system. We can't spend a lot of time training...."

You can see it's going to be a long day.

WHAT TO DO, WHAT TO DO . . .

You start with a little noodling. If you were building a real building, you'd think about

1. Use: what purposes it is supposed to serve. After all, form follows function.
2. Design: how high, wide, and deep, what characteristics it must have (doors, windows, roof), how the space must be organized inside, what plumbing and electrical codes and other external constraints apply
3. Location: where it will be, how to get there, what the site will be like
4. Organization: who's going to build it and how the job is going to be run
5. Financing: what it's going to cost and where you're going to get the money.

You can set financing aside, for the moment at least. The boss has already decided that a database is the way to go. So presumably the company has the money.

Location? A database goes on a computer, on a particular database system. You make a note: talk to the Information Technology (IT) people.

Organization? There's a tough one. Are you expected to be your own project manager? Or has one been assigned? What about staff? Who will be needed? What skill sets? Training? Methods? This needs a lot of looking into.

And so you've come to that inseparable duo, use and design, and to the fundamental question: What's the scope? What's included? What's excluded?

You've already been told what's included: your area of the business. That helps. It also helps to know a little about databases. Relational databases. A bunch of tables made up of rows and columns. So it should be enough to specify those tables, their attributes, and their relationships.

Or is it enough? And how do you do it? The big question hovers overhead:

What goes into a database design?

And out of the ether, an answer:

Database design begins with the business.

Up to this point, you'd been wondering if you're supposed to be involved at all. But, in fact, you are the essential person, and for one reason: **You know your business, what it is and what it's supposed to be.**

Imagine the database as a mirror of your business area—or, better, a painting of it. The things that exist in the real world have to be translated into images, and those images have to be arranged on the canvas. Put the right images in the right place, and your painting shows how the world is made. Wrong images, wrong places, and you've got a mess.

You know your world best. In systems development terms, you're a **subject matter expert**, and the role of a subject matter expert is to provide the business knowledge that will determine the design of the automated system. In applications development, you might be called a requirements engineer. But you're concerned specifically with database requirements: what data will be stored and what relationships among data will be established in the database.

To define the requirements for your database, you document your business knowledge by writing business planning statements. Then (with the help, usually, of at least one experienced data modeler) you formalize that knowledge in a **logical data model**. The logical data model is the design for the painting, the blueprint for the building.

Once your logical data model is built, you'll work with your database people to translate it into physical tables in the database management system and the corresponding application programs that your company will use. And when they build it, you will come, and you will test it, and you will say, "It's good. Just like the real world."

But first you have to learn how to create a logical data model. That's what this book is here to teach you.

SO WHAT IS DATA MODELING, ANYWAY?

We'll start with a quick, high-level survey of data modeling. Then we'll get on to the hard work at hand.

If your company is at all well managed (an iffy thing in itself) ...

Let's put it another way: If your company expects to survive in the race for the customer's dollar, top-level management must be doing some strategic planning. That means they have to consider things like

- Why the company exists
- What the future looks like
- Where the company wants to go
- What the company's competitive strengths and weaknesses are
- What opportunities exist for growth and profit
- What threats lurk in the shadows.

Out of this thinking come projects, priorities, projections, and targets. If, as is usually the case, this planning is done badly or not at all, serious time and money are wasted on failed projects—especially IT projects—and short-lived systems (Standish Group 1994).

The problem is to integrate **enterprise strategic planning** with **systems development** and **database design** (Finkelstein 1992: 3). If this is done, what we have is one or more **strategic information systems**. The goal of this integration is to ensure that the systems we build will provide direct support for management decision making. And the way we do that is to draw effectively and systematically on management's business knowledge and IT people's systems knowledge.

A word of warning: Even when corporate planning is done with a reasonable degree of sophistication—which means developing business models—too often it turns out to be a mere exercise. It enhances management's feelings of control, but produces nothing substantive: no priorities, no implementation, no continuing interest. We're talking management commitment here, and management willpower. How often do you find that?

Enterprise strategic planning means doing strategic, tactical, and process/operational modeling so that priority operational systems can be implemented long before all the modeling is completed. In other words, if you do your modeling right, you can be completing one project while another is still in the planning stage.

Our modeling approach is called **Information Engineering** (IE). IE uses subject matter experts like you to analyze, design, and develop systems from the business side. If you do your part right, you can be sure that the plans match the needs and that the systems *as built* match the plans. Guess how much money that saves.

Furthermore, as the systems development process goes forward, you can deal with the changes that inevitably occur. With IE, you get rapid feedback so you can modify your plans on an ongoing basis.

A more specific term for what you're doing is **Enterprise Engineering**, sometimes called "business-driven Information Engineering." EE is where the business side meets IT. It is a methodology for active collaboration between business and IT during project development. When business people and IT people know how to work together, the result is faster development and higher quality.

In the process of working up your data model, you will develop close ties with both the business-side users and the systems development team—the IT people. Your data model, reflecting the users' information requirements, will let the people in the business group communicate effectively with one another and with the database people during implementation.

Following the methodology outlined in this book, here's what you will do:

1. Collect planning statements and build formal Business Statements for your project area.
2. Identify the entities that represent the information you use and collect in that area.
3. Define the associations between the entities that you've identified.
4. Define the attributes that identify and describe information items.
5. Develop a data map.
6. All along the way, identify and correct errors in the logical data model.
7. Apply the rules of business normalization to the data model. If you build the logical data model correctly from the start, you may not need to worry much about business normalization: the completed logical data model will already be properly normalized.

Once all those things are done, you are in a position to work with the IT people to implement the data model as a database on any appropriate hardware or software platform:

- Entities will be implemented as records or tables.
- Attributes of the entities will be implemented as columns in a table.
- Associations between entities will be implemented as tables joined by common keys.

Be forewarned: there will be differences between your model and the actual, physical database. For example, some of your logical entities may become two or more physical tables, and the physical key structure may vary from the logical key structure. But that's why the Database Administrator (DBA) is there: to handle the inevitable differences.

NEW NOTIONS

subject matter expert, data modeling, logical data model, strategic information systems, Information Engineering, Enterprise Engineering

1.   COLLECTING PLANNING STATEMENTS

Your first task is to assemble all the information you can about the expectations, goals, directives, and rules that govern your project area. You'll find this information called many different things, like "mission statement," "policy," or just "what we do around here." But once you get your hands on it, it becomes a collection of **planning statements**: clear, well-structured (we hope) statements of intentions, requirements, and relationships.

To prepare you for this part of the process, we're going to discuss two things:

- What you're looking for, and why
- Where to look for it, and how.

Note: You don't have to collect *all* the relevant planning statements before you proceed to the next step in the data modeling process. In fact, as you develop your data model, you will inevitably have to seek out statements that are necessary but missing. You may even have to invent them as a logical consequence of what you've learned.

1.1   Kinds of modeling and flavors of statement

Business planning is often done formally, but it is seldom done comprehensively. Minor projects may get funded, while important projects get ignored. Efforts in different parts of the organization may be duplicated or inconsistent. Data collected locally may be useful locally but may not communicate well across divisional boundaries.

Enterprise Engineering looks at business planning as a consistent, comprehensive, continuing process that starts at the top and works down. From this viewpoint, there are three kinds or levels of modeling:

- Strategic modeling, at the enterprise (company) level
- Tactical modeling, at the division or department level

- Process or operational modeling, at the systems level.

Modeling at different levels depends on planning statements at different levels of specificity. Below, we've identified twenty-one flavors of statement[1] and arranged them in three sets, according to the different kinds of modeling and different levels of specificity. Realize that

- You can add more statement flavors if you really need to.
- You will probably use only a few of these flavors on your project.
- A particular flavor is not really restricted to a particular level of specificity. You may want to assign a statement flavor to a different level.

1.1.1 Strategic modeling

Strategic modeling discovers what areas of the business need to be developed if the company is going to implement its corporate strategy.

Here are the seven flavors of strategic planning statement. Each answers a particular kind of question. "Vision" and "Mission" are well known, but a considered strategic plan will spell out assumptions as well.

You may be familiar with the last four as **SWOT**—used for situation analysis—or as **WOTS-UP**: Weaknesses, Opportunities, Threats, Strengths Underlying Planning. Weaknesses and strengths are internal to the organization, while opportunities and threats are external.

Flavor	Question	Example
Vision	What do you see as the ultimate result of the enterprise's efforts?	"The Houston Community College System will be an integral part of the social, economic and educational life of the community through quality partnerships and responsiveness to community needs."[2]

---

[1] Or, more correctly, we've borrowed them from Visible Systems Corporation, which uses them with its Visible Advantage enterprise modeling tool.

[2] *Mission and Plan, 2000-2003* (April 26, 2000), Houston Community College System, http://www.hccs.edu/system/admin/mission20.html.

Flavor	*Question*	*Example*
Assumption	What conditions, necessary for the ongoing functioning of the enterprise, do you assume will continue into the foreseeable future?	"We are assuming 20,500 members by the end of this year. We are estimating that 18,450 members will pay an additional $25 in 2000."[3]
Mission	What have you committed the enterprise to accomplishing?	"NOAA's mission is to describe and predict changes in the Earth's environment, and conserve and wisely manage the Nation's coastal and marine resources."[4]
Strength	What resources, circumstances, and qualities give the enterprise an advantage in accomplishing its mission?	"This interdisciplinary approach, in which faculty and researchers from various academic fields form teams to conduct research, ... places Carnegie Mellon in a strong position for the future when collaboration among various fields will be key to solving the most difficult research problems."[5]
Weakness	What does a successful effort require that may not	"Lack of cohesion amongst Fellows and a perception that the College leadership is unrepresentative of the

---

[3] "Budget Assumption to Support the Year 2000 Operating Plan," *2001-2004 Strategic Plan*, Public Relations Society of America, http://www.prsa.org/_About/strategy/budget.asp?ident=strat3.

[4] *Strategic Plan: A Vision for 2005* (September 1998), p. 1, Office of Strategic Planning, National Oceanic and Atmospheric Administration, http://www.osp.noaa.gov/docs/NOAA_current_Strategic_Plan.pdf.

[5] "Cross-disciplinary Research" [1995], Carnegie Mellon Strategic Planning, Carnegie Mellon University, http://www.cmu.edu/splan/PlanProc/CrossDiscPrograms/CrossDiscplRsch.html.

Flavor	Question	Example
	be available or that you may not be able to provide?	broader Fellowship are leading to disunity."[6]
Opportunity	What opportunities exist for advancing the enterprise?	"Use of emerging technologies provides ACHP with the opportunity to expand dramatically the audience it reaches."[7]
Threat	What external forces or circumstances exist that threaten to hinder the success of the enterprise?	"The physician's time will become an increasingly scarce resource as more elements are added to the clinical encounter (e.g., discussions on advanced directives, prevention, safety), additional administrative tasks are expected (e.g., increased documentation requirements), and requirements for recertification become more extensive (e.g. Continuous Professional Development – CPD)."[8]

1.1.2 Tactical modeling

Tactical modeling identifies necessary operational systems, functional areas, or general project areas. Priorities for development are set at the tactical level.

Tactical modeling statements are more specific than strategic modeling statements, because they define directions at a lower organizational level.

---

[6] *Strategic Plan 1996-2000*, Royal Australian and New Zealand College of Psychiatrists, http://www.ranzcp.org/college/strategy.htm#7.

[7] *Six-Year Strategic Plan*, adopted 1997, amended November 2000, Advisory Council on Historic Preservation, http://www.achp.gov/plan.html.

[8] "Environmental Assessment: 2002-2007," *Strategic Plan - Fiscal Years 2002-05*, American College of Physicians - American Society of Internal Medicine, http://www.acponline.org/strategic/tando.htm.

Often, they are presented as elaborations of specific statements in the strategic plan.

The seven flavors of tactical statement are often hard to sort out. In practice, the terms "Goal" and "Objective" are often treated as synonyms or as parent and child: goals are realized by meeting a number of objectives, or vice versa. "Goal," "Objective," "Critical Success Factor," and "Strategy" may be used at the strategic level, while policy statements and tasks will be found at the process/operational level.

Flavor	*Question*	*Example*
Goal	What do you want to accomplish (at the level of functional area)? What change do you want to effect?	"It is the overall goal of EPA Region III to maintain a high state of emergency readiness and to respond immediately and effectively to all environmental emergencies which warrant an EPA presence."[9]
Strategy	How do you propose to accomplish those goals? What alternative strategies exist?	"Improve the employee evaluation process and examine appropriate compensation for staff via a classification modernization study."[10]
Critical Success Factor	What must you achieve if you expect to succeed? What will kill the project if you fail to achieve it? What measures will you use to determine success or failure?	• "Obtain computing capabilities of 2 (.2) TFLOPS. • "Move from top 50 to top 25 in Academic High-Performance Computing."[11]

[9] *Tactical Plan for Responding to Major Oil Spills* (August 2000; rev. August 2001), U. S. Coast Guard, http://www.uscg.mil/lantarea/rrt/rcp/Admin/Tacticalindex.html.

[10] "Goal 3: Professional Development," *Service and Stewardship 2001-2005*, Ohio Department of Natural Resources, http://www.dnr.state.oh.us/parks/ss/goals/goal-3.htm.

[11] *Strategic Plan*, IT Division, High Performance Computer Center, Texas Tech University, September 11, 2003, http://www.infotech.ttu.edu/strat/hpccsp.html.

Flavor	Question	Example
Objective	What milestones have you set for measuring your progress toward your goal?	"To develop undergraduate specialization in Entrepreneurship (additional to B.Sc. requirement) with Venture Development Center (VDC)."[12]
Policy	What rules of practice (i.e., rules for decision-making) must be followed in the operations of the enterprise as a matter of course?	"Computing & Networking Services will monitor in real-time, backbone network traffic, as necessary and appropriate, for the detection of unauthorized activity and intrusion attempts."[13]
Tactic	What methods are you going to use to advance toward your goal? When and how are you going to apply them?	"CRT will seek out opportunities at appropriate trade shows and conferences for representatives of the U.S. Commission to speak."[14]
Task	What actions will you take to achieve specific goals?	"Formulate and present to the North Central Accreditation Agency a proposal on standards for quality library media programs."[15]

[12] "First Year Tactical Plan," *Designing Our Future: Vision Review & Strategic Plan Enhancement* (November 1996), Faculty of Engineering, University of Calgary, http://www.eng.ucalgary.ca/design.htm#firsttarget.

[13] "Network Security Policy," Computer Security Administration (December 2000), Computer and Networking Services, University of Toronto, http://www.utoronto.ca/security/policy/.

[14] "Tactical Program," National Plan for the Centennial of Flight Commemoration (November 2001), U. S. Centennial of Flight Commission, http://www.centennialofflight.gov/commission/natl_plan/Appendix3_3_1.htm.

[15] *Futures Strategic Plan of Action* (no date), Michigan Association for Media in Education, http://www.mame.gen.mi.us/organiz/futures.html.

1.1.3 Process/Operational Modeling

The last seven flavors apply to statements written during **process modeling** or **operational modeling**. You will recognize them if you've ever participated in a business process re-engineering or systems implementation project. On the operational level, issue management systems are commonplace, and business events are identified in procedures and user manuals.

As for "business rules," they're all over the place, but they are usually collected and identified as such only during a modeling project. They state what the people who know the business know: how work gets done and why it is done that way. Companies that have done thorough strategic and tactical modeling may have formal systems for managing business rules, so that changes can be migrated to the data models and the systems that are based on those models.

Flavor	*Question*	*Example*
Business event	What events, external to the functional area, trigger action in the functional area?	"User 1. Contact the ACS Help Desk to report the problem."[16]
System event	What events, built into the manual or automated system, trigger action in the system or in functional areas external to the system?	"Before Allocation is run, the system sets the Reporting REPORT DISPLAY DATE to the last day of the prior accounting period."[17]

---

[16] *Problem Management Guidelines and Procedures* (November 1994), p. 5, Riyad Bank, Riyadh, Saudi Arabia.

[17] *System Administration Guide*, General Ledger System (November 1994), p. 22, Riyad Bank, Riyadh, Saudi Arabia.

Flavor	Question	Example
System requirement	What characteristics must the system have in order for it to perform the required functions under the given circumstances?	"Monitoring and Maintenance activities shall be done distributed at NOS level."[18]
System design objective	What functions must the system be designed to perform? What tests must we apply to confirm that the system performs those functions?	"Every chassis [must] operate within an ambient temperature range of 0° to 55°C with a maximum internal temperature rise of 20°C, when populated with enough cards to fully load the installed power supplies."[19]
Business rule	What relationships must exist within the enterprise in order for work to get done in a structured manner?	"Renter and each Additional Authorized Operator must be present to sign Rental Agreement, present an acceptable credit card (debit cards not acceptable) or current round-trip ticket (air, train or bus), show valid driver's license, and must be a minimum of 25 years of age."[20]

---

[18] "Layout of the HSTN," *Design of a Hybrid Satellite-Terrestrial Network (HST)*, ENSE 623, ENPM 643 System Engineering Design Project, University of Maryland, http://www.isr.umd.edu/Courses/ENSE623/DirecPC/layout.html.

[19] *Designing Industrial Computing Solutions for Optimal Cooling and Airflow* (no date), p. 2, Kontron/ICS Advent, http://www.kontron.com/techlib/whitepapers/5004.pdf.

[20] "Authorized and Additional Authorized Operators," Qualifications and Requirements, *Before You Rent*, Hertz, http://www.hertz.com/.

Flavor	Question	Example
Issue for resolution	What questions need to be answered? What problems need to be solved?	"Applications may fail with an access denied message from the services after successful installation of Pervasive.SQL Windows Server to a local drive."[21]
System design goal	Taken as a whole, what is the system supposed to do?	"The design goal for the SVE system was to extract a total volume of soil vapor equal to 500 pore volumes from beneath the site within 30 years."[22]

YOU ARE HERE

Or so we'll assume. Your concerns are probably at the tactical and process levels. Your area has been identified as a priority operational area for development. You know what planning statements look like, and you're ready to start collecting them.

But where to look?

1.2   Discovering planning statements

There are generally three places to look for planning statements:

- Documents
- Systems
- People.

And the greatest of these is people. But first, a few rules:

---

[21] Knowledge Base, Pervasive Software, March 2001, http://support.pervasive.com/eSupport/publisher.asp?id=96ed7bb3-195f-11d5-b230-00508b5d6b61.

[22] *Soil Vapor Extraction at the Seymour Recycling Corporation Superfund Site, Seymour, Indiana* (no date), Federal Remediation Technologies Roundtable, http://bigisland.ttclients.com/frtr/00000128.html.

1. **Test every statement against reality—that is, against actual practice or reasonable expectation.** The way people work is often at odds with the way they're supposed to work. And management has a way of blowing smoke.
2. **Test statements for clarity, consistency, and testability.** Vague statements are untestable. For details, see the standard in Section 1.5.
3. **Make sure your information is up-to-date.** Documents, especially, get real old real fast.
4. **Understand exactly what you are discovering**:
   a) The way things actually are, *OR*
   b) The way somebody thinks things should be, *OR*
   c) The way things are going to be in the future.

1.2.1 Documents

One thing to remember about documents: most of the time they're written by and for other people. That means the planning statements they contain aren't in your language and aren't written for your purposes. As you develop your data model, you're going to have to rewrite, collate, consolidate—in short, you're going to have to make the statements your own.

1.2.1.1 Strategic

The best documents for data modeling are those that come from within your company. Those most relevant to strategic planning generally originate with senior management. Many of them are concerned with defining relationships between the company and important external audiences:

- Shareholders
- Clients and customers, current and prospective
- Vendors
- Government
- Community.

Other documents result from formal planning efforts or record corporate decision-making. Some address broad internal audiences, like middle management or workers.

Flavor Set 1: Strategic	*Documents*
Vision	Strategic plans, corporate websites, shareholder
Assumption	documents, capabilities documents, employee
Mission	indoctrination documents, intranet home page,

Strength	community relations documents, forecasts,
Weakness	marketing studies, situation analysis reports,
Opportunity	budgets, corporate minutes
Threat	

1.2.1.2 Tactical

Documents relevant to tactical modeling exist on the corporate division or department level. They reflect the planning, organization, and assessment of work. They record the responses of middle management to the directions set at higher levels.

Flavor Set 2: Tactical	*Documents*
Goal	Business plans, requests for proposal, proposals,
Strategy	scopes/statements of work, forecasts,
Critical Success Factor	performance reports, minutes, organization
Objective	charts, budgets, policy manuals, management
Policy	directives, performance standards, job
Tactic	descriptions, delegations of authority, charts of
Task	accounts, project schedules, audit reports,
	tactical plans

1.2.1.3 Process/Operational

Documents on the process/operational level generally fall into three broad categories:

- Those that say what **should** occur: procedures, manuals, training materials, contracts
- Those that say what **did** occur: transaction files, reports, studies, knowledge base
- Those that are generated in the course of systems development, present or past.

Flavor Set 3: Process/Operational	Documents
Business event System event System requirement System design objective Business rule Issue for resolution System design goal	Functional requirements, system design documents, standard operating procedures, knowledge base, issue resolution reports, financial reports, performance reports, staff studies, historical reports, transaction files, master reference files, white papers, user manuals, training documents, case studies, contracts, user manuals, reference manuals

1.2.1.4 External documents

Compared with internal documents, external documents like textbooks, journal articles, and the sales materials of competitors are much less relevant to your purposes. But there are a few exceptions:

- Industry standards and best practices for your area's processes
- Industry data models and data specifications—for example, the Petroleum Industry Data Model, http://www.ppdm.org/index.html, and the Art Museum Image Consortium data specification, http://www.amico.org/AMICOlibrary/dataspec.html
- Published data models for common business functions like accounting, HR, ordering, shipping, work orders, and the like[23]
- Planning documents from organizations like your own.

These documents can suggest planning statements that may exist in your own functional area. They can speed up your effort by providing templates that you can adapt and apply. They can help you meet quality standards and make subsequent modeling projects easier.

If you are installing an ERP system (not the subject of this book), you will deal extensively with the ERP system's physical database.

1.2.2 Systems

Systems are organized ways of getting work done. Usually, they combine manual, mechanical, and automated processes. The manual component—the

---

[23] See, for example, Silverston 2001.

human factor—is defined in documents like Standard Operating Procedures. As for the rest, you'll find them in three places:

1. In your own functional area
2. In other functional areas in your company
3. In other organizations.

Start by asking yourself: What systems and system components already exist for doing the work of my area? Some of them may be so familiar as to be almost invisible: telephone, copy machine, computer workstations, office automation software, the company intranet. Others might not normally occur to you when you think about "systems": office or shop floor layout, emergency warning systems, splash showers. If it's functional, and if it's within your scope of work, you can probably start there and work backward to a policy, business event, or business rule.

If a database system has already been implemented in your area, the project documents may not have been thrown out. There you should find the system's logical and physical data models, which can be mined for useful information like entity and attribute names and specifications. Whether or not you're so lucky, nonetheless you have the user interface and outputs, and you may want to look at change, issue, and problem reports.

Some other area of your organization may have implemented a similar database. If so, you can draw on that system's implementation, user, and reference documents and on the users' experience. There are also databases in other organizations. Vendors and business partners may be able to help here. As long as you respect the other fellow's need for confidentiality, you may be able to get useful ideas about how to tackle your own problems.

And then there's the gold mine. In one organization with which we consulted, management had built a database to mine the metadata (the data about data) from all existing company databases. Every night, every database reported back on its physical tables, associations, and attributes.

1.2.3 People

In data modeling, people are much more than subject matter experts and sources of planning statements. They are the users of the database and the systems that will draw on it. If they aren't made an active part of the planning, they won't have confidence in the result or confidence in you. By involving them in the planning process, by leading them through development of the logical data model, you give them what they will need for communicating with the technical people.

The core event here is the **data modeling session**: you, an experienced data modeler, and a few users doping out the information structure on the whiteboard. Here's a quick sketch of the process:

1. You'll identify the groups you need to talk with. Sessions work best with two, three, or four people who perform the same or similar business functions.

2. You'll prepare yourself intellectually and psychologically. You'll learn as much as you can about the functional area and the methods of data modeling. You'll meet the people you'll be working with, find out about them, develop a rapport. You'll put yourself in "listening mode."

3. You'll announce the sessions: why they're being held and what will be on the agenda. But you may want to ask each participant to prepare a job description, emphasizing responsibilities, duties, tasks, and interfaces with people and systems inside and outside the business area.

4. In the initial session with each group, you'll tell them about data modeling and its role in the project. You'll make it brief and high-level—the analogy with a blueprint works well—and then you'll get to work, asking questions, listening, and sketching out the entities and associations on the whiteboard. After an hour or less, you'll send the folks home with thanks. Then you'll transcribe everything you learned and everything you wrote on the whiteboard.

5. You'll conduct extra sessions if you need them. Otherwise, you'll interview individual participants as necessary to clarify details.

6. You'll call one or more larger, follow-up meetings to present your draft data map and get feedback. You'll want to bring the participants from three or four groups together, so they can see how their work fits together in the data model.

You're probably wondering what questions you'll ask in the sessions. Don't worry. By the time you've worked through this book, you'll know.

In a perfect world, if you were building the big database in the sky and had unlimited resources, you would begin by holding sessions with vice presidents. Your resulting data model would reflect the organization at the strategic level.

Next, you would perform a technique called clustering (Finkelstein 1992: 424-437; Reingruber and Gregory 1994: 41-44), which breaks down the strategic level model into tactical areas like, for example, personnel and manufacturing. Then you would hold sessions with the directors and managers whose responsibilities relate to each individual cluster, to build tactical models.

When you finished modeling one tactical cluster, you could then start modeling a different tactical cluster or priority operational areas within the first cluster. A database for one area could be under development while tactical modeling proceeded on another cluster.

Nice job if you can get it.

1.3   New notions

planning statement, strategic modeling, tactical modeling, process modeling, operational modeling, vision, assumption, mission, strength, weakness, opportunity, threat, goal, strategy, critical success factor, objective, policy, tactic, task, business event, system event, system requirement, system design objective, business rule, issue for resolution, system design goal, data modeling session

1.4   Exercise: List your planning statements

This is a simple but very useful exercise, best done in a word processing document:

1. Write down each planning statement, one after another, in a list. No duplicates, of course.
2. If a statement asserts more than one thing, break it up into separate statements.
3. Put the statements in an approximate order. Try to place the broadest statements first, the more detailed ones below, but keep related statements together.
4. If two statements seem to be saying the same thing, but in different words, put them together and tag them for further consideration.
5. If you see any inconsistencies, tag them, and be sure to note where the conflicting statements came from.

1.5   Standard for planning statements

1. Each statement must describe the business, not the database.
2. Each statement must express one and only one fact.
3. Each statement must be unambiguous: it cannot be misunderstood.
4. Each statement must include any conditions necessary for it to be true.
5. Each statement must be properly grammatical.
6. Each statement must be in the active voice and use an action verb.
7. Each statement must use terms that are standard in your business or in the industry.
8. Terms must be used consistently throughout the entire set of statements:
   a) A word must not be used in one sense in one statement and another sense in another.
   b) Two different words must not be used to represent the same thing or idea.

2.   WRITING FORMAL BUSINESS STATEMENTS

Notice: You don't have to collect *all* the relevant planning statements before you start writing Business Statements.

Now you've collected your planning statements, you've written them down in good form, and you've developed "inside" knowledge about the area you're modeling. There's more rewriting to be done, though. To make them optimally useful for data modeling, you'll need to recast them as formal Business Statements.

Business Statements describe

- objects of interest—almost anything indicated by a noun, any category that we want to capture and keep information about:

  o Persons (not proper names, but job titles or roles)
  o Places
  o Things
  o Events
  o Concepts

- characteristics (attributes) of those persons, places, things, events, and concepts

- properties of those characteristics
- associations of persons, places, things, events, and concepts with other persons, places, things, events, and concepts
- characteristics of those associations.

Business Statements follow a stricter standard than garden variety planning statements. In particular, a Business Statement

- uses a limited vocabulary and a limited grammar: certain words or phrases and only certain sentence structures
- is of one flavor only—usually, a business rule.

Collected together, your Business Statements

- comprise a formal record of the your area's knowledge
- demonstrate that all parties—you, the users, and senior management—are in agreement
- let you model the system: most Business Statements become parts of the logical data model
- let you assess the system once it's built.

To look ahead: There will be a mapping between each Business Statement and a part of the logical data model.

Let's look at some sample Business Statements:

- Each STUDENT may register for zero, one, or many CLASS SECTIONs.
- STUDENT has the following subtypes: UNDERGRADUATE STUDENT, GRADUATE STUDENT.
- Each STUDENT has a unique student-identifier.

As with good planning statements in general,

- The sentences are all in active voice, not passive: "Each STUDENT" does something, is something, has something.
- The verbs are all in the present tense. (Statements of intention would use verbs in future tense: "Each STUDENT will eventually declare one or many MAJORs.")
- Each time the same thing is referred to, we use the same name. A STUDENT is always a STUDENT, not a PUPIL in one statement and a STUDENT in another.
- The statements are unambiguous: you can't misinterpret them.
- They are all consistent with each other.

We can easily see some other characteristics of these statements:

- The names of objects of interest are CAPITALIZED.
- The first word of most statements is "Each." (This will help us to define how our objects of interest relate to each other.)
- Each statement is of only one flavor. The first statement describes a business event. The other two statements are business rules.

2.1 Standard Forms

Following are seven Standard Forms[24] of Business Statement. They don't cover all possibilities, but they are the most immediately useful ones. Feel free to develop your own standard forms, but keep the number reasonable.

2.1.1 Standard Form I: The Basic Form

Each T1	*must* *may* *will eventually*	*<association> <quantity> T2.*

where

- *T1 and T2 identify objects of interest.*
- *<association> is a verb like "be," "have," "become," or almost any action verb.*
- *<quantity> is one of the following:*

  o *"one or many"*
  o *"zero or one"*
  o *"zero, one, or many"*
  o *"one and only one."*

In this abstract form, the statement reads: "Each instance of the object of interest may or must or will eventually have this kind of association with this amount of another object of interest." (An instance is one of the set, like Annette is one of the Dionne quintuplets.)

Let's take an example. We have a business rule that says, "Instructors will teach at least one but no more than 100 students in a semester." We can

---

[24] The way these Standard Forms are presented is not standard across data modeling practice. We've adopted this presentation because it's quick to learn and easy to use.

capture some of this knowledge in an unambiguous form by using Standard Form I:

"Each INSTRUCTOR must teach one or many STUDENTs."

In this statement,

- T1 = INSTRUCTOR
- T2 = STUDENT
- modal verb = "must"
- association = "teach"
- quantity = "one or many."

And our statement is testable: if we find an instructor who teaches no students, either the statement is wrong or that person isn't an instructor.

Notice one thing about phrasing:

- If we say that an instructor must teach, we say that he or she teaches one or more students.
- If, on the other hand, we said that the instructor may teach, we would have said that the instructor teaches zero, one, or many students. Our phrasing might be redundant, but it certainly can't be misunderstood.

2.1.2 Standard Form II: Subtypes

T1 has the following subtypes: ST1, ST2, ..., STn.

where ST1, ST2, etc., are subtypes (classification groups) of T1, the object of interest.

Another way of putting it:

Each T1 is	*one and only one* / *one or more*	*of the following subtypes:*	*ST1, ST2, ..., STn.*

Obviously, there have to be at least two STs. Otherwise, you don't have subtypes.

Here's an example of Standard Form II:

"CHANGE has the following subtypes: SIMPLE CHANGE, MODERATE CHANGE, MAJOR CHANGE."

In this case, an individual change can be of only one subtype. It can be a simple change, or it can be a moderate change, or it can be a major change.

But it can't be both a simple change and a moderate change. And a simple change can never become a moderate change, or vice versa.

Sometimes, though, we have a different situation:

"DISH has the following subtypes: APPETIZER, SALAD, ENTRÉE, SIDE DISH, DESSERT."

To clarify this situation, we need to add one or more statements in Standard Form III.

2.1.3 Standard Form III: Roles

Each STn	*may* / *must*	*also be a STm at the same time.*

where STm and STn are both subtypes of T1.

Read it like this: "Each instance of this subtype may or must also be an instance of that other subtype at the same time."

Let's look at our Standard Form II example again:

"DISH has the following subtypes: APPETIZER, SALAD, ENTRÉE, SIDE DISH, DESSERT."

To clarify, we add a statement of Standard Form III:

"Each APPETIZER may also be an ENTRÉE at the same time."

For example, you can serve quiche as an appetizer or as the main dish.

Note these details:

- We said "may," not "must," because some appetizers, like olives, won't be used as the entrée.
- To clarify our Standard Form II statement adequately, we'd have to add more Standard Form III statements, like "Each SALAD may also be an ENTRÉE at the same time."

Variants

In our example, the phrase "at the same time" doesn't mean "in the same meal." It just means that our DISH (quiche) doesn't have to cease being served as an appetizer in order to be promoted to entrée-hood. So we might want to write our statement like this:

"Each APPETIZER may also serve as an ENTRÉE."

As long as the statement is unambiguous and testable, and APPETIZER and ENTRÉE are both subtypes of DISH, we've got a useful statement.

We might want to expand our Standard Form III like this:

"Each APPETIZER may also be a SALAD, ENTRÉE, or SIDE DISH at the same time."

This is useful for completeness' sake, though, in fact, a good bit of this information will drop out at data modeling time.

2.1.4 Standard Form IV: Becoming

Each STm may eventually become a STn.

where STm and STn are both subtypes of T1.

In other words, "Each instance of this subtype may eventually become an instance of that other subtype." Like Standard Form III, Standard Form IV is used to clarify a Standard Form II (subtypes) statement.

Let's make up some good examples:

Standard Form II	*Standard Form IV*
"HUMAN BEING has the following subtypes: CHILD, ADULT."	"Each CHILD may eventually become an ADULT."
"UNION MEMBER has the following subtypes: APPRENTICE, JOURNEYMAN, MASTER."	"Each APPRENTICE may eventually become a JOURNEYMAN." "Each JOURNEYMAN may eventually become a MASTER."

Notice that in the second example we don't have an apprentice becoming a master, even though every master was once an apprentice. That's because union policy requires every apprentice to become a journeyman before he or she can qualify as a master.

2.1.5 Standard Form V: Recursion

Each T1	*must* *may* *will eventually*	*<association>* *<quantity>* *T1.*

where

- *T1 identifies an object of interest.*
- *<association> is a verb like "be," "have," "become," or almost any action verb.*
- *<quantity> is one of the following:*

  o *"zero or one"*
  o *"one or many"*
  o *"zero, one, or many"*
  o *"one and only one."*

Standard Form V is not the same as Standard Form I. Here, each instance of our object is associated with zero, one, or many instances of the same object.

For example,

- "Each TRAINER may train zero, one, or many TRAINERs."
- "Each SHARE will eventually become zero, one, or many SHAREs." (That's what happens in a stock buyback or a stock split.)

2.1.6 Standard Form VI: Characteristics

Each T1 has the exactly zero or one of the following characteristics: C1, C2, ..., Cn.

where T1 is the object of interest.

When we use Standard Form VI statements for data modeling, we'll refer to "attributes" instead of "characteristics." But "characteristics" is good enough for now.

Let's look at an example:

"Each ARTWORK has exactly zero or one of each of the following characteristics:

  o artwork-accession-number
  o artwork-artist
  o artwork-date
  o artwork-descriptor
  o artwork-genre
  o artwork-location
  o artwork-number

    o   artwork-relationship
    o   artwork-subject
    o   artwork-title."

Notice: Depending on the data modeling technique, characteristics are often presented as hyphenated suffixes to the object name and are often written in lower case.

2.1.7 Standard Form VII: Properties

C1 has the following properties: P1, P2, ..., Pn.

where C1 is a defined characteristic of T1, the object of interest.

As if it weren't obvious: a property is a characteristic of a characteristic.

Example:

"The characteristic *artwork-descriptor* has the following properties:
    o   A term used for grouping artworks
    o   Maximum 30 alphanumeric characters
    o   Not unique
    o   May repeat (maximum 5 times)
    o   May be null
    o   No default value."

2.2   The Standard Forms in action

Let's apply these Standard Forms to a strategic statement:

We hire employees who presently have none of our skills, but we will train them. Each employee must have demonstrated an ability to be trained, however. We must have at least one employee, but we need many for each skill. (Finkelstein 1992: 45)

We'll do a quick rewrite before we do our Business Statements:

* An employee may have none of our skills initially.
* We will train new employees in our skills.
* The employee must be trainable.
* For each of our skills, we need at least one employee who has that skill.
* Every skill will eventually have many employees exercising it.

Notice that there are some questions that remain unanswered. For example, how does an employee demonstrate trainability? The strategic statement, predictably, will require further analysis. That's the real world, folks.

From our rewrite, we can come up with the following Business Statements:

- Each EMPLOYEE may have zero, one, or many SKILLs.
- Each EMPLOYEE will eventually have one or many SKILLs.
- Each SKILL must be held by one or many EMPLOYEEs.

Note that all three statements follow Standard Form I. Also, each statement is of a single flavor. They are policy statements (Flavor Set 2), which derive from strategic statements.

Here's a quick look ahead:

EMPLOYEE >|---o|< SKILL

This is the first bit of the data map: "Many EMPLOYEEs will eventually be associated with one or many SKILLs." In the reverse direction: "Each SKILL must be held by at least one EMPLOYEE." That's what the notation says. We'll get into that later.

Now let's do a Business Statement in Standard Form VI:

"Each EMPLOYEE has exactly zero or one of each of the following characteristics:
- o employee-number
- o employee-name
- o employee-hire-date
- o employee-pay-rate."

Finally, let's use Standard Form VII:

"The characteristic *employee-number* has the following properties:
- o employee-number is a five digit base ten numeric field, unique to each individual.
- o An employee-number is never assigned to more than one individual.
- o Each employee will always have the same employee-number, even if he goes away and comes back several times."

Notice how close we're approaching to defining a database.

2.3 New notions

Business Statement, Standard Form

2.4 Exercise: Rewrite your planning statements as Business Statements

You have your list of planning statements from Step 1. Now rewrite as many as you can according to the Standard Forms.

1. Divide planning statements into multiple Business Statements as necessary.
2. If you can't manage to rewrite one, skip it and go on to the next.
3. Gather more information as necessary.
4. Note any issues for further inquiry.

By the time you've worked through the list, you will have

- added statements to your list.
- added depth and detail to your understanding.
- started thinking about planning statements in Business Statement terms.

Chapter 2

THE ART GALLERY WEB: A DATA MODELING EXAMPLE

Wherein Dr. Pangloss sets out to build his dream web

"Over the years, [Dr. Pangloss tells us,] I've visited lots of art museums, and at every one I bought slides and postcards of the artworks. I've scanned these items and incorporated them into a web that I like to share with my friends via CD-ROM. I dream of someday putting this web up on a secure website for educational purposes, but for right now I'd just like to create a database of all the information about these artworks. Then, when I actually have a website, I could arrange for web pages to be created on the fly.

"I started by defining the purpose of the web."

Business Description: Art Gallery Web

1. Purpose: The purpose of the Art Gallery web is to

provide the owner's friends with access to electronic images of artworks on CD-ROM and, in the future, on a secure Internet website.

"Then I gathered all the basic sources of information together. That was easy. There were only two: the existing art gallery web and me, the Subject Matter Expert. (As time went on, I regretted not having SOPs [Standard Operating Procedures], instructions, and standards to draw on.) Using these sources, I refined my business description by listing the web's functions."

2. Functional Description: The functions of the Art Gallery Web are to

a) display the images themselves, with identification (artist, title, date, location, and accession number [the museum's identifying number] if available) and comments (optional, with citations if necessary, hyperlinked to item in List of Works Cited)

b) display thumbnail images that are hyperlinked to the (larger) images

c) categorize images or thumbnails by artist (with pseudonym, if available, and dates of birth, death, and/or activity), medium, genre, era, etc.

d) provide access to images of works by an artist via a timeline (set of commented links)

e) provide access to portraits by an artist via a portraits index (set of commented links)

f) provide access to images of works by an artist via an artists index

g) display two images side-by-side, for comparison

h) list the museums represented in the collection, with URL if it exists

i) provide a list of works cited in comments (authors, title, publication date, publication location, and publisher)

j) provide a search facility (not implemented on CD-ROM)

k) provide a discussion facility (not implemented on CD-ROM)

l) describe the theory, origin, and functions of the art gallery web.

"Now I was ready to write as many business rules as I could. I didn't try to write formal business statements. I just wanted to get ideas down on paper. Often I included examples: they're quicker to record and more basic than formal definitions."

3. Business Rules

a) Each artwork is identified by artist, title, date, location, and accession number in the source collection.

b) An artwork may have no artist (= Anonymous), one artist, or more than one artist.

c) An artwork may have no date, or the date may be generalized (e.g., ca. 1640, last quarter 15th c., 1616-1630).

d) An artwork may have no current location (e.g., location unknown, destroyed).

e) An artwork may have no accession number.

f) Each artwork may be classified according to

- *artist*
- *genre (painting, architecture, stained glass, others)*
- *era (e.g., Classical Antiquity)*
- *origin (Africa, Nigeria, Yoruba, Court of Benin)*
- *current location (Kunsthistorisches Museum, Sistine Chapel)*
- *period style (Renaissance, baroque)*
- *source (Book of Kells)*
- *encompassing artwork (Birth of Venus, Allegory of Spring)*
- *group of artworks (Nine Heroes Tapestries)*
- *subject (Divine Comedy, madonnas)*
- *affinity group (Modern American Artists), etc.*

g) Artist and genre are the primary categories of classification.

h) An artwork may itself contain works of art. An altar is made of different panels, as often as not by different artists. An illuminated book may have artistic value in itself, beyond the illuminations it contains.

i) Artwork genres include paintings, sculpture, architecture, a piece of decorative art (jewelry, plate or cup, stained glass, tapestry), and other (mixed media, collage).

j) An estate or a museum may be an artwork in itself.

k) Each artist is identified by name, pseudonym (optional), and dates of birth, death, or activity.

- *Most artists have only a name, no pseudonym.*
- *Some artists are known only by pseudonym (e.g., Boucicault Master).*
- *Some "artists" are known only by association with a named artist (Workshop of Filippo Lippi, Follower of Rogier van der Weyden).*
- *For some, we have no date of birth; for some, we have no date of death; for some we have a year or span of years in which the artist flourished or was active.*

l) An artist might also be the subject of comments from a cited work, but this is not implemented.

m) Each artwork has zero or one current location. That location may be a private collection (Mrs. Virginia Kraft Payson), a museum (Louvre), an estate (Versailles), or a building (Lenbachhaus, Palazzo Vecchio).

n) A current location is identified by country, city, and name. But it may also be a collection in a museum, a room in a building (Chapel of Eleanora di Toledo), a building on an estate (Petit Trianon), even a surface (Sistine Chapel ceiling).

o) A museum or estate may have a website.

p) An artwork may have one or more comments.

q) A comment may have one or more citations (links to reference works).

r) A reference work is identified by author, title, publication date, place of publication, and publisher. It may also have a volume number, series name, etc.

s) Each artwork is shown in one or more images. An artwork usually has only one image. But there may be other images of the artwork that are different in visual quality or source, or that show the artwork in relationship to other artworks, or that show a detail of the artwork.

t) Each image has zero or one thumbnail.

u) Each image has a filename.

v) Each thumbnail has a filename that relates it to its corresponding image.

"As I worked on the data model, other business rules occurred to me, and I added them to the list."

[Dr. Pangloss doesn't yet feel ready to write formal Business Statements. But he'll get there. *To be continued* ...]

Chapter 3

BUILDING THE DATA MAP

Wherein we start making sense

Once we've got a reasonable number of Business Statements, we're *almost* ready to start data mapping. Here's what we're going to do:

1. Identify entities
2. Define associations
3. Classify entities by flavor
4. Build the data map (first draft)
5. Define primary and foreign keys
6. Relate keys to associations
7. Validate cardinality and optionality of associations
8. Validate associations on the data map
9. Define attributes
10. Verify the data model
11. Validate the data model against the rules of normalization
12. Revise, revise, revise.

Of course, when you get good at this stuff, a lot of these steps will collapse into each other, and you'll be revising constantly, moving your understanding closer and closer to reality.

1. IDENTIFY ENTITIES

Look at your Business Statements. Those words in CAPITAL LETTERS are the names of **entities**: collections of things that are important to your company, things that (in the abstract world of data modeling) represent *data that needs to be stored for reference.*

Let's get a little deeper into the definition:

1. In the real world, we use nouns to name classes, groups, or collections of things. We use the word "cow" to designate a whole bunch of similar animals. Similarly, in the data model for a college we can use STUDENT as the name for students as a group—in fact, all students who are or have ever been registered at the college.

2. If we want to identify a particular cow or student, we will often use a proper name: "Elsie" or "Eberhard Faber." In data modeling terms, the individual things that make up the entity are called **instances**: Elsie is an instance of "cow," and Eberhard is an instance of "student" (the group). Each instance of an entity is unique, just as Elsie and Eberhard are unique. And many instances make up an entity: you will never have an entity that has just one instance for very long.

3. But the world of data modeling is a little more abstract. As an entity in the college's data model, STUDENT represents a collection of structured data about students, and each instance of STUDENT is a set of particular data about a particular student: name, address, GPA, etc.[25] Because our friend Eberhard is unique as a student, he is represented as a unique instance of the data entity STUDENT.

4. If you want to get philosophical about it, an instance of STUDENT can be said to exist only as a subset of the data defined by the data entity STUDENT: a student can be recognized as an instance of STUDENT only by exhibiting the attributes of the entity. This is why a virtual student can attend classes, take exams, and even graduate (as happened some years ago) and why a student without a student ID is not, functionally, a student.

Notice that the name of an entity is

- a noun (i.e., the *name* of a person, place, thing, event, concept, etc.)
- expressed in the singular, not in the plural
- your company's term for that important thing

---

[25] We might have applied the term "entity" to the individual persons, places, or things, and then used the term "entity set" to designate the group, class, or genre that those "entities" belong to. We *might* have done things this way. But that terminology isn't common in the field of data modeling, so we'll stick with the more standard usage of "entity."

- unique within the data model.

In the world of data, an entity *may* eventually become a table in a real information system. Its characteristics—called **attributes**—then become columns in that table. And the instances of the entity—data about real things like people, purchase orders, or products—populate rows in that table. We do not put actual people, purchase orders, or products into the rows of the table. That's impossible. We put information about entities into tables.

The first thing we're going to do is create rectangles: one rectangle for each entity. So, for example,

represents the entity STUDENT—unique and unchanging—in all the Business Statements where it occurs.

1.1 New notions

entity, instance, attribute, entity rectangle

1.2 Exercise: Create an entity roster

Here's a simple starting point:

1. List the capitalized nouns in all your Business Statements.
2. Write a definition for each.
3. Go back over your collection of business rules, pull out any other nouns that might represent entities, and list them.
4. Beside each one, if it doesn't look like an entity, explain why it isn't an entity.
5. If you find a new entity, write one or more appropriate Business Statements for it.
6. Save the lists, definitions, and explanations in your project folder.

Congratulations! You now have a basic entity roster, you have clarified your thinking about the problem, and you have a record of that thinking: something that you will find useful to refer to later on, as you revise the data model.

2.   DEFINE ASSOCIATIONS

When all the entity rectangles are strung together with the proper kinds of **associations**, the result is a **data map**. A data map is like an organization chart for information. It shows the structure of data in the functional area.

Here are two general rules for associations:

- A connection between two entities is always meaningful. The different possible meanings are shown, according to data mapping conventions, by different kinds of connectors.
- No entity is an island. Each rectangle must be connected to at least one other rectangle on the map—which is to say, every entity must have at least one association with another entity in the data model.

Now let's look at the basic connections:

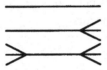

These are also called **association lines**. The first means **one-to-one**, the second means **one-to-many**, and the third means **many-to-many**.

So, if we see this—

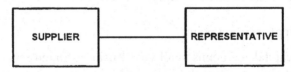

—we read it as "Each instance of SUPPLIER relates to <u>one and only one</u> instance of REPRESENTATIVE, and vice versa."

If we see this—

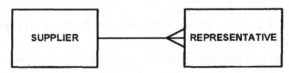

—we read it as "Each instance of SUPPLIER relates to one or more instances of REPRESENTATIVE." Or, if we read from right to left: "Each instance of REPRESENTATIVE relates to exactly one instance of SUPPLIER."

Finally, if we see this—

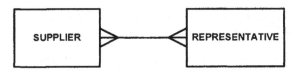

—we read it as "Each instance of SUPPLIER relates to one or more instances of REPRESENTATIVE, and each instance of REPRESENTATIVE relates to one or more instances of SUPPLIER."

These are the only three kinds of connection that are allowed. However, you may have occasion to use a connector like this:

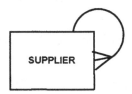

This indicates a **recursive** association. In other words, "Each instance of SUPPLIER may relate to one or many instances of SUPPLIER." Recursive associations are expressed using Standard Form V.

So here are our two rules about association lines:

- Each association line associates *exactly two* entity rectangles.[26]
- The association expressed by an association line runs in both directions, from Entity 1 to Entity 2, and from Entity 2 to Entity 1. The association can be expressed in words in both directions.

There are also a couple of "modifiers" that indicate whether the connection is

- *mandatory* (Entity 1 must have a relationship with Entity 2. Or, in other words, each instance of Entity 1 must have a relationship with at least one instance of Entity 2.) *OR*
- *optional* (Each instance of Entity 1 may have a relationship with zero, one, or many instances of Entity 2.) *OR*
- *optional-becoming-mandatory* (Each instance of Entity 1 will eventually have a relationship with one or more instances of Entity

---

[26] As we'll see, it's useful to think this way about the curved line in a recursive association. We might imagine rewriting the example above to look like this: SUPPLIER >---< SUPPLIER.

2. An instance may not currently have the relationship, but it will acquire that relationship at some time in the future.).

The *mandatory* relationship is indicated by a short line (|) crossing near the end of the basic association line at right angles, like this:

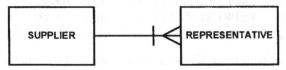

This means: "Each instance of SUPPLIER *must* relate to one or many instances of REPRESENTATIVE."

If we replace the short line with a circle (o), we indicate that the relationship is *optional*, like this:

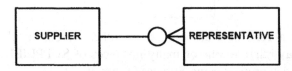

Which is to say: "Each instance of SUPPLIER may relate to zero, one, or many instances of REPRESENTATIVE."

And if we put the two together (o|), we indicate *optional-becoming-mandatory*.

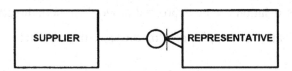

In English: "Each instance of SUPPLIER must eventually relate to one or more instances of REPRESENTATIVE."

We say that these modifiers indicate the **optionality** of the association. And when we talk about the **cardinality** of the association, we're talking about whether an entity has a one-to-one, or a one-to-many, or a many-to-many association with another entity.

Whatever their optionality, one-to-many relationships are often called *parent-child relationships* and will get implemented in associated tables— that is, tables connected to each other by a shared key. Mandatory-one-to-mandatory-one relationships usually get resolved into a single entity, so they're easy to implement as a single table.

It's the many-to-many relationships that give us trouble. Implemented directly in a relational database, they might require n-dimensional tables, and the computer space required might just multiply geometrically each time we add a new relationship. But there is a solution:

Reduce all many-to-many and recursive associations to one-to-many relationships.

That is going to be our goal from here on out as we create our data map.

2.1 New notions

data map, association, one-to-one, one-to-many, many-to-many, recursive, mandatory, optional, optional-becoming-mandatory, optionality, cardinality, association line

2.2 Exercise: Create an Entity-Entity Matrix

An Entity-Entity Matrix is a way of making sure that you consider all possible pairs of entity instances.

1. Take the entities identified in your entity roster—for example,
   o ARTWORK
   o ARTIST
   o IMAGE
   o LOCATION
   o REFERENCE

—and create a table that shows all the possible pairs of entities, like this:[27]

	ARTWORK	ARTIST	IMAGE	LOCATION	REFERENCE
ARTWORK					
ARTIST					
IMAGE					
LOCATION					
REFERENCE					

---

[27] For reasons of space, we've omitted the secondary entities. But they're legitimate entities, and they should be there.

2. In each cell, describe the relationship (if any) between the column entity and the row entity. Use Business Statement terms: *may, must, will eventually*, etc. Your descriptions should read from left to right, row by row:

	ARTWORK	ARTIST	IMAGE	LOCATION	REFERENCE
ARTWORK	may contain 0, 1, or many	must be created by 1 or many	must be shown in 1 or many	must reside in 1 and only 1	may be described in 0, 1, or many
ARTIST	must create 1 or many	may work with 0, 1, or many	(1)	[none]	(2)
IMAGE	must show 1 and only 1 (3)	[none]	may be related to 0, 1, or many	[none]	[none]
LOCATION	must contain 1 or many	[none]	[none]	[none]	[none]
REFERENCE	must describe 1 or many	[none]	[none]	[none]	[none]

3. Each time you make a judgment call, make a note of it. For example:
   (1) "We will not be tracking images of artists (e.g., self-portraits)."
   (2) "We will not be tracking comments about artists, only about artworks."
   (3) "A few images show two artworks for comparison purposes, but we will not track them."
4. Make a list of all the associations in your table. Then validate them by matching each one to a specific Business Statement. If you have any Business Statements left over, or if a Business Statement is related to a great number of associations, that may tell you something. (Note: Some enterprise modeling tools can generate the report you need. If you're making your own, you'll find this process easier if each of your Business Statements is in one of the Standard Forms.)

An Entity-Entity Matrix is okay for small projects. But, obviously, the more entities you have, the larger the table. That's why for larger projects it may be better to use an enterprise modeling tool. But creating an Entity-Entity Matrix has its advantages. It reminds you to

- Be thorough
- Document your decisions

- Check for errors in Business Statements
- Validate your work.

As you learn more about entities and associations, you will find it useful to go back to your Entity-Entity Matrix and revise it to reflect your current understanding of the area you are modeling.

Another way to check for correctness is to build a Statement-Entity Matrix. Here's part of a matrix created using the Visible Systems' Visible Advantage enterprise modeling tool:

Data Objects ⟶ Statements	ARTIST	ARTIST COMMENT	ARTIST STRUCTURE	ARTWORK	ARTWORK ARTIST	ARTWORK COMMENT	ARTWORK
ARTIST ALPHABETICAL LISTING (Business Rule)							
ARTIST DATE STRUCTURE (Business Rule)							
ARTIST IDENTIFICATION (Business Rule)							
ARTIST RELATED TO ARTIST (Business Rule)							
ARTIST RELATED TO ARTWORK (Business Rule)						√	
ARTIST RELATED TO COMMENT (Business Rule)		√					
ARTIST TIMELINE (Business Rule)							
ARTIST TIMELINE (Business Rule)							

The items on the left are the titles of the Business Statements. (The flavor of the Business Statement is given in parentheses.) The items across the top are names of entities. The associations between Business Statements and entities are marked at the intersections. If you find that a row or column contains a great number of associations or no associations, something may be wrong.

3. CLASSIFY ENTITIES BY FLAVOR

Now you're *almost* ready to start connecting entity rectangles. Here are all the flavors of entities you'll be connecting, along with the symbols we'll be using:

- Principal (P)
- Secondary (S)
- Intersecting (I)
- Type (T)
- Role (R)
- Structure (U)

If it helps any, you can juggle the symbols to spell U-STRIP or STIR UP.

3.1 Principal Entity

A **principal entity** is of interest to the entire enterprise—for example, EMPLOYEE. After all, every area in the company has employees.

To put it another way, a principal entity usually crosses organizational boundaries. For example, the principal entity STUDENT is used both in scheduling classes and in billing.

For later discussion, we'll indicate a principal entity as "P". On the data map, it will be a rectangle like this:

```
┌─────────────────┐
│                 │
│    STUDENT      │
│                 │
└─────────────────┘
```

P entities come in two varieties: dynamic and static. Mostly, we'll be concerned with dynamic P entities. These entities, when converted into tables in a database, contain data which changes frequently. For example, STUDENT and EMPLOYEE are both dynamic P entities: students are constantly enrolling, dropping out, or graduating; employees are being hired, fired, laid off, etc.

Static P entities, on the other hand, can be thought of as lists that don't change very often, such as a list of states in the union (e.g. Alabama, Alaska, Arizona, Arkansas, etc.). Static P entities are different from dynamic P entities in certain ways.

From here on out, you can assume that we are discussing dynamic P entities unless we say otherwise. We'll discuss static P entities a little later.

3.2 Secondary Entity

A **secondary entity** is a subtype of a dynamic principal entity. In terms of databases and stored information, it is a way to collect and store certain information that is (1) related to a dynamic principal entity, but (2) of interest only to one or two parts of the enterprise.

For example, the dynamic principal entity EMPLOYEE may have a secondary entity called SALESPERSON that is of interest to Sales, but not, probably, to the currency trading floor. In a relational database, the SALESPERSON table would hold information that describes employees in the Sales Department. And it won't hold all the information on those employees, but just the information of interest to that department.[28]

Secondary entities don't come alone. If a dynamic principal entity has any secondary entities at all, it must have at least two, and they must be distinct. Each secondary entity usually contains information different from its mates.

In discussion, we'll represent secondary entities with "S". On the data map, a secondary entity looks like a box on an organization chart:

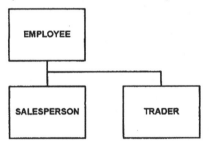

Otherwise, a secondary entity acts like a dynamic principal entity: it can have associations with other entities—principal, secondary, role, type, and intersecting—and it can have subtypes of its own. We'll discuss this later.

---

[28] You may need to define a secondary entity in order to keep certain information secure, available only to people who are authorized to have it. Maybe the Sales Department doesn't *want* other departments to know the details of its sales force.

3.3   Intersecting Entity

Here's a typical many-to-many association between dynamic principal entities:

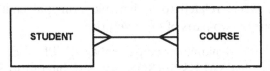

In other words, one student may take many courses, and one course may be taken by many students.

The way we handle this association is to create a new, "artificial" entity (a **meta-entity**) called an **intersecting entity**:

STUDENT COURSE is an entity that cross-references students and courses. It can also hold other useful information as well: attributes like the semester when the course was taken and the grade the student got.

There are a couple of other many-to-many associations that an intersecting entity can resolve:

1. Between a dynamic principal entity and another dynamic principal entity's associated secondary entity, and
2. Between two secondary entities each associated with a different dynamic principal entity.

Here's an example of the first case. We have a many-to-many association between the dynamic principal entity MATERIAL and the secondary entity SPORTS, which is a subtype of the principal entity SHOE. We are saying that a sports shoe can be constructed of a number of different materials and that a material can be used in many different sports shoes. (We are also saying that, for whatever reason, we don't care about materials used in dress or casual shoes—not a realistic assumption, but we are trying to make a point here.)

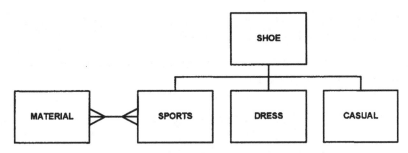

We can resolve this association by creating the intersecting entity SPORTS MATERIAL:

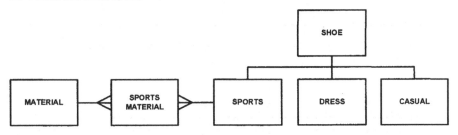

As for our second case, a many-to-many association between secondary entities of different parents, well, we'll leave that to you to sketch out an example.

For convenience, we'll often indicate an intersecting entity as "I".

3.4 Type Entity

Defining the relationship between a dynamic principal entity and its secondary entities starts with creating a meta-entity called a **type entity**, which later we'll indicate as "T".

Let's say we have the following Business Statement:

Each ARTWORK has the following subtypes:

- o *PAINTING*
- o *SCULPTURE*
- o *ARCHITECTURE*
- o *DECORATION*
- o *OTHER*

In this case the association between the dynamic principal entity (sometimes called the **supertype**) and all of its subtypes, taken together, is such that an individual artwork may be any of these things, but it is one and only one of them.[29] These five subtypes cover all artworks we're interested in (anything that doesn't fit elsewhere qualifies as "other").

We would start out by drawing the association between the dynamic principal entity and the secondary entities:

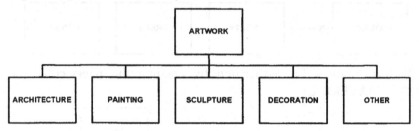

Then we create a type entity and place it in our map like this:

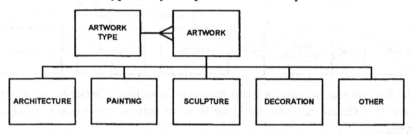

Notice that the connector between ARTWORK TYPE and ARTWORK indicates *one-to-many*. We can read the diagram like so: "Each instance of ARTWORK TYPE describes one or more ARTWORKs, and each ARTWORK is of exactly one ARTWORK TYPE," i.e., is a work of ARCHITECTURE, a PAINTING, a SCULPTURE, a DECORATION, or a work of some OTHER type.

One thing about our list of artwork types: it covers the world. Anything that isn't a work of architecture, a painting, a sculpture, or a decoration is automatically of type OTHER, and secondary entities like PHOTOGRAPH or DRAWING could be added later if necessary. There is, however, another way of handling artworks of unidentified type. We can define a Type 0 (zero) and associate that type with the principal entity, ARTWORK itself.

---

[29] The relationship between the supertype and *any one particular instance* of a subtype is *mandatory-one-to-optional-one* (P -|---o- S): in other words, an instance of the supertype may relate to zero instances or one instance of that particular subtype.

Then, if we have to classify a photograph or a drawing or some such, we associate it with Type 0.

The type entity may become a table in a relational database. It must have at least two attributes (columns): artwork type number and artwork type name. In words and spelling (but not necessarily capitalization), **the "artwork type name" must exactly match the name of the corresponding subtype entity: "painting," "architecture," etc., not "picture," "building," and the like.** So our ARTWORK TYPE table would look something like this:

artwork_type_no#	artwork_type_name
1	architecture
2	painting
3	sculpture
4	decoration
5	other

Or, if we used the "Type 0" option,

artwork_type_no#	artwork_type_name
0	artwork
1	architecture
2	painting
3	sculpture
4	decoration

A type entity is always indicated by adding "TYPE" to the entity name: EMPLOYEE TYPE, STUDENT TYPE, etc.

3.5 Role Entity

Now let's look at another Standard Form II business statement:

Each ORGANIZATION has the following subtypes:
   o *CUSTOMER*
   o *CONTRACTOR*
   o *SUPPLIER.*

In this case, the association between the supertype and all of its subtypes is *many-to-many.*[30] An individual organization can be a CUSTOMER, or it can

---

[30] Whether this association is *mandatory-many-to-mandatory-many* or *mandatory-many-to-optional-many* depends on whether or not the subtypes, taken together, cover all instances.

be (or can become) a CONTRACTOR. ABC Pest Control can have a pest control contract with Monsanto and at the same time buy its pesticides from Monsanto.

This many-to-many relationship marks these subtypes as **roles**. That means they get some extra treatment.

We start just as before:

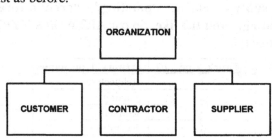

Then we add the type entity:

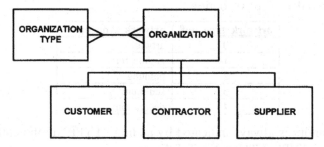

Notice that the association between ORGANIZATION and ORGANIZATION TYPE is many-to-many: an organization may have many types, and each type may have many organizations.[31]

Now here's where the **role entity** comes in:

If each instance of the dynamic principal entity must have a subtype, the association is mandatory in that direction. These issues will be covered more thoroughly when we discuss **optionality** and **valid associations**.

[31] If the association between the type entity and the dynamic principal entity is one-to-many, we have an *exclusive* type entity: an instance of the dynamic principal entity can be of one and only one type. If, on the other hand, the association is many-to-many, we have an *inclusive* type entity (Finkelstein and Aiken 2000: 98-99).

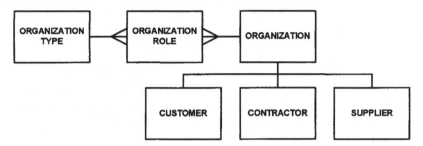

The association between ORGANIZATION and ORGANIZATION ROLE is one-to-many, and so is the association between ORGANIZATION TYPE and ORGANIZATION ROLE. We can read it like this: "Each organization has one or more organization roles, and each role has one organizational type."

Notice that the role entity is like an intersecting entity between the dynamic principal entity and the type entity. We can expect it to function similarly, as a cross-reference between the dynamic principal entity and its corresponding type entity.

One last thing. A type entity can be associated with only one dynamic principal (or secondary) entity. In other words, it can define the subtypes for only one supertype. If you introduce a role entity, it sorts out the relationships between the supertype entity and its type entity: between those two entities and no others.

In later discussion, we'll refer to a role entity as "R".

3.6 Structure Entity

The **structure entity** is used to clarify situations where only specific instances of an entity relate to instances of the same entity. In other words, it's used to straighten out recursive associations.

Let's look at a recursive association:

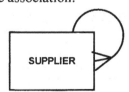

What the picture says is this: Some suppliers are just suppliers, while others have suppliers of their own.

To straighten this out, we'll create a structure entity like this:

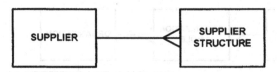

This may seem inane right now, but we will get a better understanding of it when we discuss the *keys* that identify instances in the structure entity. Later on, we'll refer to structure entities with "U".

3.7   New notions

principal, intersecting, secondary, type, role, structure, supertype, subtype, meta-entity

4.   BUILD THE DATA MAP (FIRST DRAFT)

Now let's get down to building our data map:

1. Create a rectangle for each principal and secondary entity.
2. Connect the rectangles with the proper connector: one-to-one, one-to-many, many-to-many.
3. Add the modifiers: optional, mandatory, optional-becoming-mandatory.
4. String everything together in a data map that shows all entities and associations simultaneously. For example:

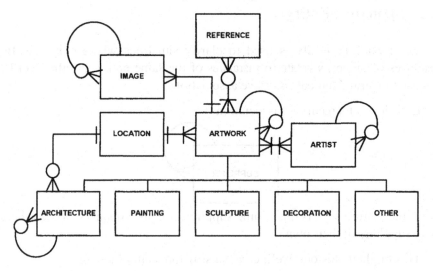

(You may find it useful to look at the relationships in the sample Entity-Entity Matrix and see how they're mapped here.)

5. Create all necessary meta-entities (intersecting, type, role, and structure). You should end up with something like this:[32]

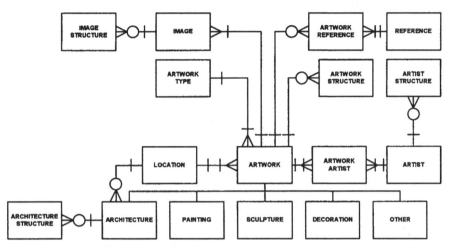

(Try reading each association on this map and comparing it with the corresponding association on the previous map.)

Usually, an enterprise modeling tool like Visible Advantage, ERwin, or Rational Rose would be used to automate the process of creating a data map. But to use them, you need to be a bit farther along in the data modeling process. For now you may find it easiest to use Microsoft Visio, Adobe Illustrator, or SmartDraw.

---

[32] This is an early draft, and it has a couple of errors. You should be able to spot them once you cover **Keys and Structure Entities** (Chapter 5, Sec. 2.8) and **Triads** (Chapter 9, Sec. 2).

(You may find it useful to look at the relationships in the sample Entity-Entity Matrix and see how they're mapped here.)

5 Create all necessary meta-entities (intersection, type, role, and structure). You should end up with something like this:

(Try reading each association on this map and comparing it with the corresponding association on the previous map.)

Finally, an alternate modeling tool like Visible Advantage, ERwin, or Rational Rose would be used to automate the process of creating a data model. But to use them, you need to be a bit farther along in the data modeling process. For now, you may find it easier to use Microsoft Visio, Visio, Illustrator, or SmartDraw.

Chapter 4

THE ART GALLERY WEB (CONTINUED)

Wherein Dr. Pangloss builds his first draft data map

[Dr. Pangloss continues:]

"Based on the business rules and the shape of my existing web, I created a first-draft list of entities, defined each, and gave a reason for inclusion. I chose the names to be close to the names I'm used to, yet clear and unambiguous. I wanted them to be one word each, so that when I created type, role, and structure entities, I would be dealing with two-word entity names. And, of course, I wanted to avoid words that are commonly reserved for doing things with databases, e.g. create, table, foreign, primary, key."

4. Initial Entity List

ARTWORK - an object that has been identified as having aesthetic value; the essential content of the site

ARTIST - the creator of an artwork. Almost all artwork images are classified and accessed via artist.

IMAGE - a visual representation of an artwork, realized as a computer file in one of a limited number of image formats; the essential means of content delivery

LOCATION - the place where the artwork resides; essential for establishing the identity of the artwork

REFERENCE - a book or other source of information about artworks, artists, and the subjects of art; a less important entity, necessary for documenting comments

PAINTING - an artwork realized by placing pigments on a (usually flat) surface; the great majority of artworks in the collection

SCULPTURE - an artwork realized in three dimensions; a very few artworks in the collection

ARCHITECTURE - art realized in a building or space; a few artworks

DECORATION - an artwork realized as an object of utility; a few artworks

OTHER - an artwork realized in unconventional or composite media and otherwise unclassifiable; few or no artworks currently; required for comprehensiveness

"I also listed the losing candidate entities and gave the reason why I was rejecting them. From my experience with software implementation projects, I knew that rare events are best left to work-arounds. This was my usual reason for omitting something. But I wanted a record of my original thinking in case I decided later that there was a good reason to add one of these candidates to the entity list."

Rejected as entities

artwork title, date, and collection accession number - attributes of ARTWORK

era, period style - attributes of ARTWORK. These might eventually become entities, depending on how important the concepts are

origin - may be an entity (because there are multiple levels of origin definition); but rarely used, therefore low priority

source - ambiguous: could mean either a "source artwork" or a non-art "source medium"

group of artworks - rare

encompassing artwork - handle by recursive relationships

subject - multiple values for one artwork; possible multi-level; low priority for implementation as an entity

museum, building, estate - covered in LOCATION and ARCHITECTURE

website - attribute of some current locations

comment - an attribute of ARTWORK; the same comment will not usually be used to describe two different artworks; the citation pointing to REFERENCE can be made an attribute of ARTWORK as well

thumbnail - an IMAGE; best to think of it as one of two images related to an artwork, than as an image related to another image

filename - attribute of IMAGE

"There are lots of mistakes in these lists. I realize that now. But I had enough to go on, and so I created an Entity-Entity Matrix. I wanted to record the relationships between the entities, and I wanted to make sure I didn't leave any relationships out."

5. Entity-Entity Matrix

	ARTWORK	ARTIST	IMAGE	LOCATION	REFERENCE
ARTWORK	contains 0/1/m	is created by 1/m	is shown in 1/m	resides in 1	is described in 0/1/m
ARTIST	creates 1/m	works with 0/1/m	(6)	--	(6)
IMAGE	shows 1 (7)	(6)	is associated with 0/1/m	--	--
LOCATION	houses 1/m	--	--	contains? (1)	--
REFERENCE	describes 1/m	(6)	--	--	--
PAINTING	is a type of	*is created by*	*is shown in*	*resides in*	*is described in*
SCULPTURE	is a type of	*is created by*	*is shown in*	*resides in*	*is described in*
ARCHI-TECTURE	is a type of	*is created by*	*is shown in*	*resides in*	*is described in*
DECORA-TION	is a type of	*is created by*	*is shown in*	*resides in*	*is described in*
OTHER	is a type of	*is created by*	*is shown in*	*resides in*	*is described in*

	PAINT-ING	SCULP-TURE	ARCHI-TECTURE	DECOR-ATION	OTHER
ARTWORK	*may be a*	*may be a*	*may be a*	*may be a*	*may be a*
ARTIST	*creates*	*creates*	*creates*	*creates*	*creates*
IMAGE	*shows*	*shows*	*shows*	*shows*	*shows*
LOCATION	*houses*	*houses*	houses 0/1/m	*houses*	*houses*
REFERENCE	*describes*	*describes*	*describes*	*describes*	*describes*

	PAINT-ING	SCULP-TURE	ARCHI-TECTURE	DECOR-ATION	OTHER
PAINTING	--	--	resides in 0/1/m (8)	may be part of 1 (2)	--
SCULPTURE	--	--	resides in 0/1/m (8)	may be part of 1 (3)	--
ARCHITECTURE	may contain 0/1/m	may contain 0/1/m	may contain 0/1/m (8)	may contain 0/1/m	may contain 0/1/m
DECORATION	may contain 0/1/m	may contain 0/1/m (2)	resides in 0/1/m (8)	may contain 0/1/m (4)	--
OTHER	--	--	resides in 0/1/m (8)	may be part of 0/1 (5)	--

"Wherever I had to make a decision about a relationship, I made a note of it in a standard format: question, reasoning, conclusion. I added the cardinality (0/1/m) to the matrix at a later stage of development, after I'd written formal Business Statements. As I updated the matrix, I added notes as necessary, numbering them in parentheses in the matrix."

***Entity-Entity Matrix Notes** [selections]*

1. Can a LOCATION contain a LOCATION? Yes. For example, the Chapel of Eleanor of Toledo is contained in the Palazzo Vecchio, and both are LOCATIONs. An artwork may be in the Palazzo, but not in the Chapel. But some artworks are in the Chapel and therefore in the Palazzo. LOCATIONs are nesting but never overlapping: an artwork cannot be simultaneously in the Palazzo and the Louvre. Therefore, by linking an artwork to the most proximal location (the Chapel of Eleanor of Toledo), we link it necessarily to all locations above it (Palazzo Vecchio). Conclusion: LOCATION is recursive....

6. There are cases of artists being shown in artworks and therefore in images, but that is of low priority. Ditto comments about artists. Conclusion: Omit these associations.

7. In rare cases, an image will show more than one artwork. Conclusion: Omit. ...

"In the Entity-Entity Matrix I put some relationships in italics. That was to remind me that those relationships were the same for the artwork type as they were for artworks in general. In other words, an artist creates a painting, but that's because an artist creates an artwork.

"Using italics that way allowed me to highlight the unusual situation: Each LOCATION houses zero, one, or many ARCHITECTUREs. The persistent problem in the data model has been how to handle situations where one artwork is part of another artwork which itself is a location—for example, when you have a sculpture by Michelangelo residing in the Palazzo Vecchio, or, better, when you have that sculpture in a particular room in the Palazzo, and that room is itself a work of architectural art.

"When I came to write formal Business Statements—and later, as I revised them—I chewed on this problem again. As usual, I kept notes about the reasoning behind each decision I made."

6. Business Statements

Each ARTWORK may contain one or many ARTWORKs. *(Assumes that a lone artwork does not contain itself.)*

Each ARTWORK must be created by one or many ARTISTS. *(Assumes that a work by an unknown artist will be associated with an artist called "unknown" or "anonymous.")*[33]

Each ARTWORK must be shown in one or many IMAGEs.

Each ARTWORK must reside in one and only one LOCATION. *(Assumes that a work that has been destroyed will be associated with a current location called "destroyed.")*

Each ARTWORK may be described in one or many REFERENCEs.

Each ARTWORK has the following subtypes:
  - PAINTING
  - SCULPTURE
  - ARCHITECTURE
  - DECORATION
  - OTHER.

Each ARTIST may work with one or many ARTISTs.

Each IMAGE may be associated with one or many IMAGEs.

Each LOCATION may contain one or many LOCATIONs.

---

[33] *and* Each ARTIST must create one or many ARTWORKs. *(Added to 3rd draft data map.)*

[Business Statements that were subsequently deleted have been omitted here.]

Each LOCATION must have one or many ARTWORKs. *(Note: This was overlooked in the Entity-Entity Matrix. I have rethought the matrix to include cardinality.)*[34]

"The advantage of formal Business Statements over the Entity-Entity Matrix is that they include optionality. So now I had everything I needed to create my data map. But I wanted to go at things systematically, so I formalized the entity-entity associations, cardinality, and optionality in a table. I underlined a couple of associations that I still had questions about. Much later, I marked out associations that I'd decided were not valid."

7. Binary Associations

Association	Cardinality	Optionality
ARTWORK --- ARTWORK	ARTWORK ---< ARTWORK	ARTWORK ---o< ARTWORK
ARTWORK --- ARTIST	ARTWORK >---< ARTIST	ARTWORK >|---|< ARTIST
ARTWORK --- IMAGE	ARTWORK ---< IMAGE	ARTWORK ---|< IMAGE
ARTWORK --- LOCATION	ARTWORK >--- LOCATION	ARTWORK >|--- LOCATION
ARTWORK --- REFERENCE	ARTWORK ---< REFERENCE	ARTWORK ---o< REFERENCE
	[subtypes deleted later]	
ARTIST ---- ARTIST	ARTIST ---< ARTIST	ARTIST ---o< ARTIST
IMAGE --- IMAGE	IMAGE ---< IMAGE	IMAGE ---o< IMAGE
LOCATION --- LOCATION	LOCATION ---< LOCATION	LOCATION ---o< LOCATION
LOCATION --- ARCHITECTURE	LOCATION ---< ARCHITECTURE	LOCATION ---o< ARCHITECTURE

"And then I built it."

---

[34] *Added to 3rd draft data map.*

8. First Draft Data Map

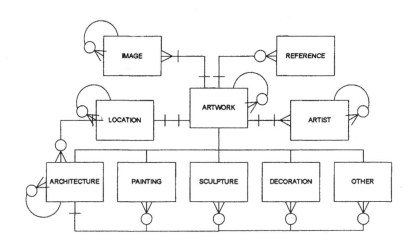

[*To be continued ...*]

Chapter 5

KEYS AND VALID ASSOCIATIONS

Wherein we acknowledge kinship

1.   DEFINE PRIMARY AND FOREIGN KEYS

Now we're in position to discuss some essentials in more detail:

- keys
- cardinality and optionality
- valid associations.

We'll start by defining a **parent-child relationship** as a one-to-many association. The parent is on the "one" end, and the child is on the "many" end. Exceptions:

1. A PS association (dynamic principal entity to secondary entity) is a parent-child relationship even though it is one-to-optional-one. That's because the one-to-many relationship is between the principal entity and *all* its secondary entities, taken together.
2. Mandatory-one-to-optional-one   (-|---o-)   and   mandatory-one-to-optional-becoming-mandatory-one (-|---o|-) are also parent-child relationships. In both cases, it's immediately clear which entity (the one on the mandatory-one end of the association) is the parent entity and which is the child entity.

Depending on its flavor and where it appears in the data map, an entity may be a parent, a child, or both a parent and a child. The notion of the parent-child relationship is a very important one, especially when we talk about keys and inheritance.

So let's talk about **keys**. If you are familiar with databases, you know about keys already.

1.1 Primary Key

When we talk about the **primary key**, we mean the attribute or set of attributes that uniquely identifies each instance of the entity. Let's take an example:

- STUDENT is an *entity*. It represents all the students in the college, in terms of the information the college gathers about them.
- *Attributes* of the STUDENT entity may include things like name, address, telephone number, graduation date, and declared major. (Note that shoe size is not an attribute: it may describe the student, but it's not information the college cares about, collects, and stores for reference.)
- If we want to identify a student uniquely—that student and no other—we don't use the student's name: who knows how many James Johnsons are on campus? Instead, we use the Student ID, because one and only one student has that number. That means that Student ID is the *primary key* for the entity STUDENT.

Notice that the Student ID is not a feature of the student as a human being. It's not a name, an address, shoe size, or anything like that. It was created solely to be the unique identifier. When a student registers for the first time, he or she is issued an ID card with a Student ID on it. From then on, that's how the college knows that particular student for any administrative purpose.

If a primary key exists for an entity, it's usually obvious what it is—for example, an employee ID number. Sometimes, though, there are two or more attributes that, taken together, identify the entity uniquely. You can then define a **compound primary key** as the combination of those attributes.

Here are a few rules for designating a primary key:

- Avoid using dates[35], text, street addresses—things that change, things that aren't obviously sequential. One common exception: email addresses. Websites often use the email address as a primary key to designate a person uniquely.
- Avoid using attributes that aren't under your company's control. Your supplier's part number may look enticing as a key. But what happens if the supplier decides to change its part numbering scheme? Or if a different supplier uses that same part number?
- If you're going to create a primary key, make it numeric: long enough for comprehensiveness, short enough for convenience. For example, a four-digit number (0000-9999) should be enough to identify all procedures in a small company.
- When you come to create an **entity list** (a list of entities and their associated attributes), write the attribute like this: <u>procedure no</u>#. By underlining the name and adding the hash mark (#), you indicate that it's all or part of the primary key for the entity.

Let's try another example. In the art gallery data model, we have an entity called ARTIST. Currently, we identify artists by the following attributes:

- Name
- Pseudonym
- Dates.

None of these can be the primary key. Two artists may have the same name—"Unidentified," for example. Not every artist has a pseudonym, as did Paolo Caliari ("Veronese"). And we don't always know the birth date or death date of an artist.

But we can see that William Morris (1834-1896) and William Morris (1957-) are two different artists, so why can't we just define name+dates as the compound primary key? Well, that would mean that we'd have key values like "Enguerrand Quarton fl. 1444-1466" and "Petrus Christus act. 1444, d. 1472/73." That's an awful lot of complication (and not easy to implement in a database). We'd do better to create a primary key called <u>artist no</u>#. If we make it a four-digit serial number, we can accommodate 10,000 artists in our gallery.

---

[35] Unless you have a good reason. See the end of **Keys and Role Entities** (Sec. 2.6, below).

A primary key like <u>student id#</u> or <u>artist no#</u> is called an **originating primary key**. That's because the key is not taken over from another source, but exists in or is created for that entity. It may help if you imagine a data entry system. Whenever you create a new record, you enter (or the system creates) a primary key value that is stored in a particular table. That key may be used elsewhere in the database, but it originates in that table. Of course, non-originating primary keys do exist, in secondary, intersecting, and structure entities in particular.

1.2 Foreign Key

Now let's relate keys to parent and child entities. A child is connected to its parent by the parent's primary key. The parent entity instance's primary key copies down to the child entity as a **foreign key**, appearing in the child entity's attribute list. That's how the child entity instance is linked to the particular instance of the parent entity that is relevant to it.

A foreign key is an attribute that does not originate with the entity itself, but is passed down from another entity. In the entity list, when we come to write the foreign key, we will write it with the hash mark (#), but we won't underline it (unless it's also all or part of the child entity's primary key). So, usually, a foreign key will look like this: artist_no#.

For example, let's take this association:

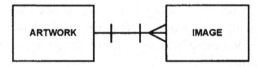

IMAGE is a child entity to ARTWORK: a work of art may have many images, but an image will be of only one work of art (a one-to-many relationship). In the entity list for ARTWORK, its primary key appears as <u>artwork no#</u>. But in the entity list for IMAGE, we will find an attribute relating the image to that work of art: artwork_no#. It's a foreign key but not part of the primary key, so no underlining.

A couple of quick tables may clarify. Here's ARTWORK:

<u>artwork no#</u>	artwork_name
1	Madonna and Child

And here's IMAGE:

<u>image no#</u>	artwork_no#
1625	1

In other words, Image No. 1625 shows Artwork No. 1, Madonna and Child.

Let's review by going back to first principles. The primary key artwork_no# lets us

- identify each artwork uniquely and
- access the information about that artwork that is contained in the ARTWORK table in our database.

The foreign key "artwork_no#" appears in the table that relates to images. It identifies the artwork shown in the image. It's a foreign key because it doesn't originate in the IMAGE table, but in the ARTWORK table. If an artwork is added to our collection, its row is added to the ARTWORK table. Then that row's primary key will be copied into the IMAGE table so that additional information about the artwork can be stored there.

1.3   Summary to this point

- Every instance of an entity has a unique primary key.
- The primary key may be simple (consisting of a single attribute) or compound (consisting of two or more attributes).
- Every instance of a child entity has one or more foreign keys copied down from its parent entity or entities.
- A foreign key may or may not be all or part of the child entity's primary key.

1.4   Identifying and Non-identifying Associations

If the foreign key (the parent's primary key) is all or part of the child's primary key, then we call the association between the parent entity and the child entity an **identifying association**, because it identifies each instance of the child entity.

For example, an out-of-state student isn't a different person from a student, so, whether she's dealing with the Registrar or with the Finance Office, she identifies herself with the same Student ID. In data modeling terms, the secondary entity OUT-OF-STATE STUDENT has the same primary key as its parent, the dynamic principal entity STUDENT. In an identifying association, the key that is copied down to the child entity is both a primary key and a foreign key.

But if the child's primary key does *not* include the parent's primary key, the child's attributes will still include the parent's primary key as a foreign key. Then the relationship between parent and child is called a **non-identifying association**. The parent entity's key still copies down, but it does not become all or part of the child's primary key.

1.5 New notions

parent-child relationship, primary key, entity list, compound primary key, originating primary key, foreign key, identifying association, non-identifying association

1.6 Exercise: Create an entity list for your data map

1. Create a three-column table and populate the left-hand column with the names of all the entities shown in your current-draft data map.
2. For each entity, write its primary key in the second column. Be sure to underline it and append the hash mark (#). If you can't determine the primary key right now, leave the space blank.
3. Hold onto this list until you've reviewed **Relate Keys to Associations** and **Validate Cardinality and Optionality of Associations** (Secs. 2 and 3, below).

    Example:

Entity	Primary Key	Foreign Keys
IMAGE	filename#	
REFERENCE	reference_no#	
LOCATION	location_no#	
ARTWORK	artwork_no#	
ARTIST	artist_no#	
ARCHITECTURE	artwork_no#	
PAINTING	artwork_no#	
SCULPTURE	artwork_no#	
DECORATION	artwork_no#	
OTHER	artwork_no#	
ARTWORK ARTIST		
ARTWORK REFERENCE		
ARTWORK TYPE		
IMAGE STRUCTURE		
ARTWORK STRUCTURE		
ARTIST STRUCTURE		
ARCHITECTURE STRUCTURE		

2. RELATE KEYS TO ASSOCIATIONS

Obviously, if we're going eventually to construct database tables from our data modeling information, we've got to provide enough of the right kind of information to make that possible.

2.1 Keys and Dynamic Principal Entities

First of all, let's consider dynamic principal entities. A principal entity (whether dynamic or static) has an originating primary key: a key of its own that it passes down to its children, if any.

A dynamic principal entity can be a parent to

- another dynamic principal entity (P), but not to a static principal entity, as we'll see
- a role entity (R)
- a secondary entity (S)
- a structure entity (U) or
- an intersecting entity (I).

In other words, there can be a one-to-many relationship between a dynamic P and any of these other entities. Remember that a dynamic P has a one-to-many relationship with *all* its related S entities. The relationship between a dynamic P and a single child S entity is one-to-one. A dynamic P can also have a mandatory-one-to-optional-one (or optional-becoming-mandatory-one) association with another dynamic P.

We've already seen these relationships in our definitions of the other flavors of entities. And we already know that the dynamic principal entity's primary key is replicated in each of its children.

A dynamic principal entity can also be child to a type entity in an exclusive subtype association. If a type entity is created to explain the subtypes of a principal or secondary entity, it is always associated with the corresponding dynamic principal entity or secondary entity in a one-to-many (parent to child) relationship. (That's by definition.) Because the type entity is the parent, its primary key will be replicated as a foreign key in the corresponding dynamic principal or secondary entity.

2.2   Keys and Static Principal Entities

We have just described the key structure for the principal entities you will use when you are dealing with what we have been calling "dynamic" principal entities: principal entities containing data subject to frequent change. Occasionally, you'll want to model "static" principal entities. The difference is that the actual data contained in static entities changes only rarely.

For example, a list of states in the union (Alabama, Alaska, Arizona, Arkansas, and so on) is not likely to change very often. As you develop your data map, you may determine that an ADDRESS entity should include an attribute for state (as in state of the union). Rather than listing all the valid values as part of the description for the state attribute within the ADDRESS entity, you can specify an entirely new static principal entity called STATE.[36]

A *static* principal entity can be a parent to any flavor of entity, even to a type entity. The primary key of a static principal entity copies down to its child entity in a non-identifying association: the static principal entity is merely supplying information, not controlling the creation of new instances in the child entity.

2.3   Keys and Secondary Entities

We already know two things about secondary entities:

- A secondary entity is a subtype to a dynamic principal entity. That means it is a child entity.
- A secondary entity can have its own subtypes (in which case it has characteristics of both a dynamic principal entity and a secondary entity). That means it can be a parent entity.

As a child to a supertype parent, the secondary entity will usually inherit its primary key from its parent. For example, if PAINTING is the child of ARTWORK, well, every painting is an artwork. Therefore, all or part of PAINTING's primary key is inherited from its parent: the relationship between ARTWORK and PAINTING is identifying. The relationship is also

---

[36] For more about attributes, see Chapter 7.

categorizing: it breaks down the instances of the parent entity into categories that are represented by all the child entities.

If a secondary entity is a grandchild (the subtype of a subtype), things get more complicated. We'll get to this situation in a minute, after we discuss the key structures for intersecting, type, and role entities.

2.4 Keys and Intersecting Entities

An intersecting entity, as you'll recall, resolves many-to-many associations between dynamic principal entities (between P and P), between secondary entities (between S and S), and between certain dynamic principal and secondary entities (between dynamic P and S). It is always the child in these relationships, and it is rarely the parent to any other entity.

The primary key of an intersecting entity is usually a compound primary key made up of the primary keys of the two or more entities it connects. For example, in this map

STUDENT COURSE is the intersecting entity. If STUDENT's primary key is <u>student id#</u> and COURSE's primary key is <u>course no#</u>, then STUDENT COURSE has <u>student id#</u>, <u>course no#</u> as its primary key. In other words, each instance of STUDENT COURSE will be uniquely identified by a student's ID number and a course number. Both associations—with STUDENT and with COURSE—are identifying.

Notice, though, that if we do things this way, we couldn't allow a student to retake a course, because we can't have more than one instance of STUDENT COURSE that has <u>student id#</u>, <u>course no#</u> as its primary key. So, instead, we should define a primary key called <u>student course no#</u> and keep "student_id#" and "course_no#" as foreign keys. In this case, both associations are non-identifying and STUDENT COURSE is redefined as a dynamic principal entity.

We could handle the situation another way. We could keep the identifying associations with STUDENT and COURSE, but add another column to the primary key—for example, a column for recording the semester or quarter during which the student took the course (F2005, etc.).

Consider this business rule: "Each student must take one or more courses in a semester." With a little information, interpretation, and logical expansion, we get the following Business Statements:

1. "Each STUDENT must take one or many COURSEs."
2. "Each COURSE accommodates one or many STUDENTs."
3. "Each COURSE is given in one or many SEMESTERs." This is from the published class schedule.
4. "Each SEMESTER provides one or many COURSEs." This is from the same published class schedule, just from a different direction.

In our notation,

STUDENT >|---|< COURSE

COURSE >|---|< SEMESTER

An obvious solution would be to create two intersecting entities and produce something like this:

STUDENT ---< STUDENT COURSE >---COURSE---< COURSE SEMESTER >--- SEMESTER

But this doesn't fit our original business rule: it doesn't relate the student to the course taken *in a particular semester*.

Actually, it maps like this:

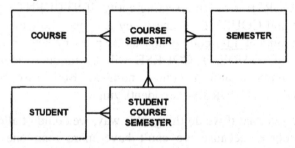

STUDENT COURSE SEMESTER is the intersecting entity between STUDENT and COURSE SEMESTER, and its primary key looks something like this:

student id#, course no#, semester#

2.5   Keys and Type Entities

We already know that the type entity is always the parent in the T-to-dynamic-P or T-to-R parent-child relationship, so its (originating) primary

key is passed to the dynamic principal or associated secondary entity as a
foreign key:

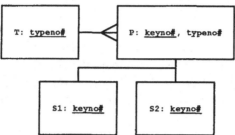

The type entity provides the dynamic principal or secondary entity with
an attribute—the foreign key shown here as typeno#—that is used to
categorize the instances of the dynamic P. It's useful to think of typeno# as a
pointer: it tells us where to find further information about a particular
instance, based on the instance's category. We follow a trail:

- In the dynamic P, we use <u>keyno#</u> to find the instance we're
  interested in.
- We look at typeno# to find out which S holds the information we
  want.
- We go to that S, look up our instance by <u>keyno#</u>, and read the
  information.

Read on.

2.6 Keys and Role Entities

When the type entity is part of a role relationship, it's still a parent, and
the role entity is the child. Likewise, the role entity is child to the dynamic
principal (or secondary) entity in the relationship:

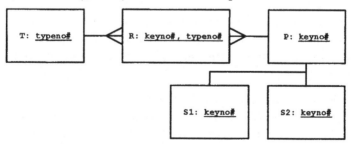

We've said that role entities are very much like intersecting entities. Like
an intersecting entity, a role entity's primary key is (usually) a compound

primary key, created by combining the primary keys of its parents. Since P is no longer child to T, it no longer has T's primary key as a foreign key.

To summarize:

- T defines the various types of secondary entity. It assigns a name (literally) to each subtype of the principal entity.
- Each instance of the dynamic P has (or may have) two or more types (i. e., subtypes, represented by the secondary entities, but defined by T) associated with it.
- Each instance of R relates an instance of the dynamic P to a particular type.
- P and T each have an identifying relationship with R: the primary key of each is copied down and becomes part of R's compound primary key.

Check this out:

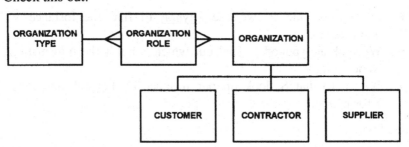

In this example, ORGANIZATION ROLE has the primary key organization no#, organization type no#. If we search ORGANIZATION ROLE, looking for the organization number of XYZ Company, we'll find one or more instances, and each instance tells us how XYZ Company relates to us: as a customer, or as a contractor, or as a supplier. The partial key organization type-no# gives us this information. Furthermore, because it's part of the primary key, it distinguishes one instance from the next. Having found all the instances related to XYZ Company, we can then home in on XYZ Company in its role as customer and find information about XYZ in that role.

We said that the dynamic principal entity and the type entity each have an identifying relationship with the role entity. Nonetheless, as with an intersecting entity, we can give ORGANIZATION ROLE an originating primary key (and make it into a dynamic principal entity). That's useful when an organization can have more than one role relationship with an organization type.

And it can happen. For example, let's say you have a business rule that says an organization can't be both a customer and a contractor at the same time. XYZ Company might be a customer, then a contractor, then a customer again. By creating an originating primary key, you can define two different ORGANIZATION ROLE instances relating XYZ Company to its role as customer. Alternatively, you could add a third key column to the foreign keys inherited from ORGANIZATION and ORGANIZATION TYPE—for instance, a column for storing a "role_start_date."

2.7 Keys and Mixed Secondary/Principal Entities

Now we're prepared to discuss what we'll call a "mixed secondary/ principal entity"[37]: a secondary entity that has child secondary entities of its own. It's a child with respect to its parent, and it functions like a dynamic principal entity with respect to its own secondary entity children. For simplicity's sake, we're not going to distinguish it as a seventh flavor of entity, but we're going to note it as S/P.

To see how the keys copy down, let's look first at the unmixed case, the dynamic-PSS association:

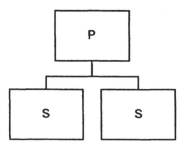

We know that in each case S has the same primary key as the dynamic P. To define the relationship between the dynamic P and S, we create a type entity:

---

[37] A principal entity with secondary entities is sometimes called a *typed principal entity*, and a mixed secondary/principal entity is sometimes called a *typed secondary entity*. ("Typed" means, of course, that an associated type entity defines the child secondary entities.)

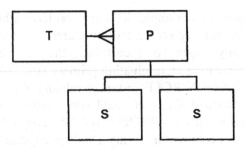

The T-dynamic-P association is non-identifying. T's primary key is copied down to P as a foreign key.

Now let's imagine that one of the secondary entities has its own secondary entities:

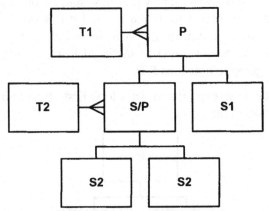

The associations P -|---o- S1 and P -|---o- S/P are identifying and categorizing: the parent's primary key becomes all or part of each child's primary key, and each association is mandatory-one-to-optional-one. The same is true for the association between S/P and S2: identifying and categorizing. In both cases, the child copies down the parent's primary key as its own primary key.

With that information, we can give the keys in detail:

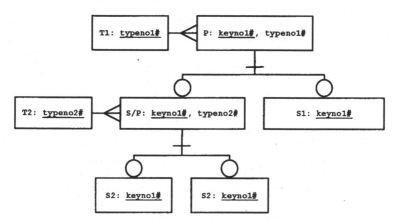

Let's follow the trail:

1. Starting at P, we use <u>keyno1#</u> to find the instance we're interested in.
2. When we find it, typeno1# tells us the instance's category.
3. If the desired instance is in S1, no problem. We look for the <u>keyno1#</u> we want, and we find the information that S1 has been holding for us.
4. If, however, the desired instance is recorded in S/P, we find that it's still identified by <u>keyno1#</u>, but it has a foreign key as well: typeno2#.
5. S/P may give us some information about the desired instance. But typeno2# tells us which S2 contains more specific information.
6. When we reach the right S2, we use <u>keyno1#</u> to find the information held there.

There is theoretically no limit to the number of parent/child levels you can have. But if you have more than three levels, something is probably wrong.

2.8 Keys and Structure Entities

We already know that a structure entity handles recursive relationships: it relates instances of a dynamic principal or secondary entity to other instances of that same entity. In a data map

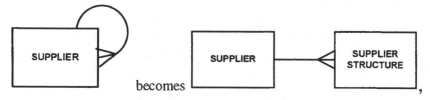

which shows that a structure entity is always a child entity.

Now here's how a structure entity actually works. Imagine that instead of writing a recursive relationship like this—

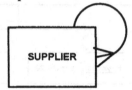

—we wrote it like this:

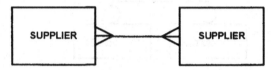

This makes sense: we're relating instances of SUPPLIER to instances of SUPPLIER. Because SUPPLIER is just one entity, we have to make the picture symmetrical, so we show the association as many-to-many.

If we saw the relationship written like this, we'd know exactly what to do. We'd create an intersecting entity called SUPPLIER SUPPLIER and put it between the two SUPPLIER entities, like this:

And because SUPPLIER SUPPLIER is an intersecting entity, it inherits the primary keys of both its parents. If we assume that the association is identifying, then SUPPLIER SUPPLIER has a compound primary key: supplier_no# (1), supplier_no# (2), where (1) and (2) indicate the different instances of SUPPLIER.

Of course, there's only one SUPPLIER entity, and there's no such thing as SUPPLIER SUPPLIER. Instead, we have

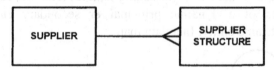

And SUPPLIER STRUCTURE inherits two supplier numbers from SUPPLIER. The first identifies one supplier in the relationship. The second identifies the other. Taken together, the two supplier numbers uniquely identify a relationship between the two suppliers. If we add a non-key

attribute to name the kind of relationship, we've got the minimum information we need to understand any instance of the structure entity.

And that's how the structure entity works:

- It receives two copies of the parent entity's primary key.
- Both copies become parts of its primary key.

2.8.1 Secondary entities and structure entities

So far, so good. Now let's complicate matters. A recursive relationship often occurs when you want to relate instances of secondary entities. For example, SUPPLIER and CUSTOMER are both subtypes of ORGANIZATION, and you want to keep track of relationships between a supplier and a customer.

First, let's review what you already know about structure entities and secondary entities:

- A structure entity records the relationship between two (usually different) instances of the same entity. The structure entity inherits two copies of its parent's primary key, one for each instance, and that's where it gets its compound primary key.
- The relationship between a supertype and its subtypes is defined by creating a type entity.
- A role entity records the relationship between an instance of a type entity and an instance of a principal entity.
- The instances of a subtype—the rows in a secondary entity—can be regarded as a subset of its parent's instances.

Next, let's review a couple of definitions:

- An *exclusive* type entity has a one-to-many association with the supertype entity: T ---< P.
- An *inclusive* type entity has a many-to-many association with the supertype entity: T >---< P. It is resolved by interposing a role entity: T ---< R >--- P.

We need these two definitions because they define two different situations that we may encounter when we have recursive relationships between instances of subtypes:

- *Exclusive*: Each instance of the dynamic principal entity has (at the most) only one type.

- *Inclusive*: An instance of the dynamic principal entity may have more than one type (either at the same time or at different times).

Case 1: Exclusive type relationship

Here's a general example of the exclusive type. You have a dynamic principal entity called ORGANIZATION. Its instances are of different types that are important to you—say, customer, supplier, and contractor.

You want to add a structure entity because, as we said before, you want to store information about the relationship between a supplier and a customer, a supplier and a supplier, a customer and a customer, etc. So let's look at our data map:

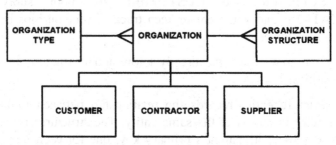

And here's how the parent/child associations work:

1. CUSTOMER, CONTRACTOR, and SUPPLIER each inherit the primary key of ORGANIZATION as their own primary keys.
2. The association between ORGANIZATION and ORGANIZATION STRUCTURE is identifying. ORGANIZATION STRUCTURE receives two copies of ORGANIZATION'S compound primary key, one for each instance that will be associated. Each of these copies (call them 1 and 2) becomes part of ORGANIZATION STRUCTURE's compound primary key.

In sum,

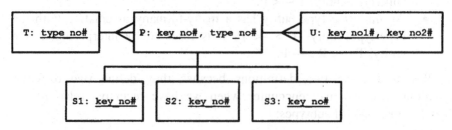

In an exclusive type relationship, an organization may be a customer or a supplier, but not both at the same time. And having been defined as a supplier, the organization can never become a customer.

So here's your customer, Booch Chemical, and you want to relate Booch to Rumbaugh Applications, one of your contractors. You have a type entity and a dynamic principal entity in your database:

type_no#	type_name
0	organization
1	customer
2	contractor
3	supplier

key_no#	type_no#	key_name
1	1	Booch Chemical
2	2	Rumbaugh Applications
3	0	Date & Codd Funds
4	3	Reasonable Software

You've also got three secondary entities, CUSTOMER, CONTRACTOR, and SUPPLIER:

key_no#	(other)
1	
7	

key_no#	(other)
2	
5	

key_no#	(other)
4	
9	

Note: **(other)** stands for other columns of information that you are using to describe organizations of a particular type.

Finally, we have a structure entity:

key_no1#	key_no2#	(other)
1	2	
2	3	

The first instance in this table relates Booch Chemical to Rumbaugh Applications. The second relates Rumbaugh Applications to Date & Codd Funds. And so it goes.

Nothing much to say here: Booch Chemical is always type 1, Rumbaugh Applications is always type 2, and there will always be only one relationship between Booch Chemical and Rumbaugh Applications. The primary key for each instance of the structure entity is unique, as it must be.

Case 2: Inclusive type relationship

In an inclusive type relationship, an instance of a dynamic P may be in more than one category (S entity), whether at the same time or at different times. Thus, there is a many-to-many association between the dynamic P and T, and this association is resolved by a role entity. If we didn't have to worry about recursion, we'd have a data map like this:

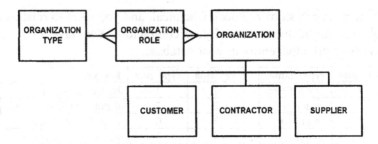

But how to handle recursion? Where to place the U entity?

The relationship we want to record is the relationship between two instances of a dynamic P *when they are associated with particular categories*—in other words, in particular roles. We get this result by placing the U entity like this:

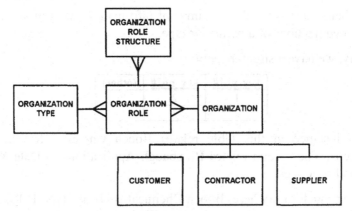

And here, in the abstract, is how the keys work:

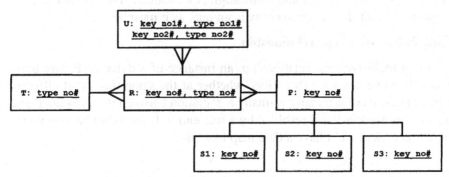

Because the role entity is child to the dynamic P and T entities, it inherits a foreign key from each, and these two foreign keys become parts of R's compound primary key. The U entity relates two instances of R. Therefore, it inherits two copies of R's primary key, one for each instance in the relationship.

So let's get back to our example and look at the tables involved, starting with the type and principal entities:

type_no#	type_name
0	organization
1	customer
2	contractor
3	supplier

key_no#	key_name
1	Booch Chemical
2	Rumbaugh Applications
3	Date & Codd Funds
4	Reasonable Software

The secondary entities contain instances of the primary entity. Because Booch Chemical has both a customer role and a contractor role and Rumbaugh Applications has both a contractor role and a supplier role, the same instance of the dynamic P will appear in two different S tables:

key_no#	(other)
1	
7	
14	

key_no#	(other)
1	
2	
4	

key_no#	(other)
2	
5	
13	

The role entity relates the organizations to their various types:

key_no#	type_no#	(other)
1	1	
1	2	
2	2	
3	0	
4	2	

And so we come to our structure entity:

key_no1#	type_no1#	key_no2#	type_no2#	(other)
1	1	2	2	
1	2	2	2	
2	2	3	0	
2	2	4	2	

Notice how the instances of R are repeated as parts of the compound primary key in instances of U. The first instance in this table relates Booch Chemical *as customer* to Rumbaugh Applications *as contractor*. The second relates Booch Chemical *as contractor* to Rumbaugh Applications *as contractor*. The third (same as in the previous example) relates Rumbaugh Applications *as contractor* to Date & Codd Funds. Again, each compound primary key is unique.

A final note: We haven't considered the possibility that Booch Chemical might be a supplier in 1999, a contractor in 2000, and a supplier again in 2001. That is to say, we might want to distinguish between Booch's relationship with Rumbaugh in 1999 and its relationship with Rumbaugh in 2001. If there are going to be more instances than one of Booch as supplier, we've got to find a way to distinguish them.

We might do this by adding an additional key attribute to the primary key in ORGANIZATION ROLE. And that means that the primary key of the structure entity will have six parts. It may not be pretty, but all the parts are necessary and everything will work. Test it out.

Another solution would be to create a static P entity called, perhaps, YEAR (assuming that roles change only on December 31 at midnight). Then we could copy down the YEAR entity's key to the ORGANIZATION ROLE STRUCTURE entity. The key for ORGANIZATION ROLE STRUCTURE would thus have five parts.

2.9   Summary: Logical inheritance of keys

Flavor	Can be a Parent to	Can be a Child to
Principal (P)	P, R, S, U, I, T[1]	T, P, S
Intersecting (I)	I	P, S, I
Secondary (S)	S[2], P, R, U, I	T, P, S
Type (T)	R, P, S	P[1]
Role (R)	U	T, P, S
Structure (U)	None	P, S[3], R

[1] A dynamic principal entity cannot be a parent to a T entity. A static principal entity can be a parent to a T entity.

[2] A secondary entity that is parent to another secondary entity is in fact a mixed secondary/principal entity if both secondary entities descend (ultimately) from the same parent.

[3] A structure entity can be a child to a pure secondary entity or a mixed secondary/principal entity, but the association will probably be handled at the top level, in a dynamic-PU association.

2.10 New notions

categorizing association, key attribute

2.11 Exercise: List the associations in your draft data map

1. Make a two-column table. In the left-hand column list every pair of entities on your data map, and in the right-hand column show the association in terms of entity flavors, like this:

Association	Flavor
ARTWORK --- IMAGE	P --- P
IMAGE --- IMAGE STRUCTURE	P --- U
ARTWORK --- ARTWORK TYPE	P --- T
ARTWORK --- REFERENCE	P --- P
etc.	

Make sure that the parent entity (usually a dynamic principal entity) is the left-hand entity in each pair. If you can't tell which entity should be on the left, well, that's something you'll have to work on. (Look at the third item in the list above.)

2. Add the "crow's foot" on the "many" side of each one-to-many association, using the "<" character:

Association	Flavor
ARTWORK ---< IMAGE	P -|---< P
IMAGE ---< IMAGE STRUCTURE	P -|---< U
ARTWORK >--- ARTWORK TYPE	T -|---< P
ARTWORK ---< REFERENCE	P -|---< P
etc.	etc.

Notice that the third item in the *Flavor* column has been revised to place the parent entity on the left.

3. Save this list of associations until you've reviewed **Validate Cardinality and Optionality of Associations** (Sec. 3, below).

3. VALIDATE CARDINALITY AND OPTIONALITY OF ASSOCIATIONS

Now that we understand keys (mostly), let's take a closer look at **cardinality** (also known as "degree") and **optionality** (also known as "nature" or "kind"). Cardinality refers to the one-to-one, one-to-many, or many-to-many character of the association. Optionality refers to its mandatory, optional, or optional-becoming-mandatory character.

Here's the basic rule:

Each valid association has exactly one strong mandatory "one" on the parent side.

That "strong mandatory 'one'" is the "Each" in Business Statements like "Each STUDENT must have one or more SHOEs."

3.1 One-to-One and One-to-Many Associations

There are three possible kinds of one-to-one associations:

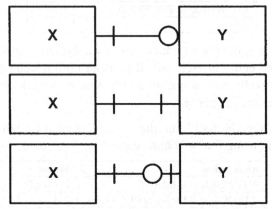

In other words,

- Each X *may* relate to exactly one Y.
- Each X *must* relate to exactly one Y.
- Each X *will eventually* relate to exactly one Y.

Likewise, there are three one-to-many associations:

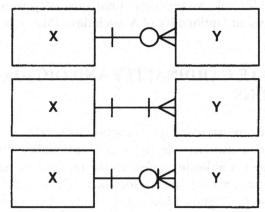

In other words,

- Each X *may* relate to zero, one, or many Y. (= "Each X must relate to zero, one, or many Y.")
- Each X *must* relate to one or many Y.
- Each X *must eventually* relate to one or many Y. (= "Each X may relate to zero Y right now, but will relate to one or many Y over time.")

3.2 Many-to-Many Associations

So what about many-to-many associations? As we already know, many-to-many associations are unimplementable in relational databases. So we resolve them using an intersecting entity. Here are the flavors of many-to-many association:

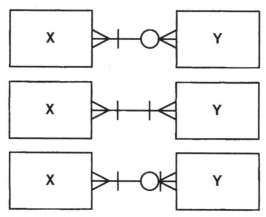

We've already seen the second association:

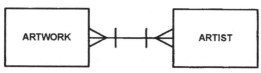

And we know how to resolve it:

But how do we handle the first association, the one with the "optional many"? Well,

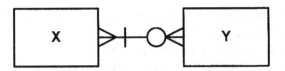

becomes

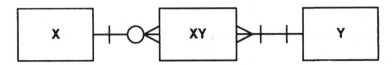

where XY represents the intersecting entity.

Let's look at this map again:

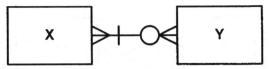

We know that the intersecting entity is the child of both of the original entities. We also know that there must be a strong mandatory "one" on the parent side. So we can decompose our map into

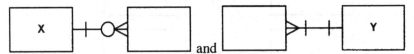 and

Entity X has a mandatory-one-to-optional-many connection with a child entity. Entity Y has a mandatory-one-to-mandatory-many connection with a child entity. And the child entity is the same in both cases: the intersecting entity. So when we put the two pictures together, we get

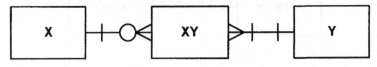

Let's try this on an example:

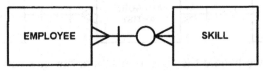

This means that some employees have no skills, some have one, and some have many, but for every skill we've identified, there must be at least one employee who has it. In Business Statement terms, "One or many

EMPLOYEEs may have zero, one, or more SKILLs, and one or more SKILLs must be associated with one or more EMPLOYEEs."

We decompose this into

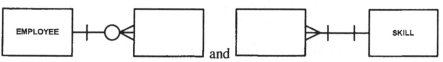

and

"Each employee may have zero, one, or more *instances of an unknown entity.*"

and

"Each skill must be associated with one or more *instances of an unknown entity.*"

So when we put Humpty Dumpty back together again, we get

This reads: "Each employee may have zero, one, or many employee skills, and each skill must be associated with one or many employee skills (i.e., skilled employees)."

Exercise: Resolve a many-to-optional-becoming-mandatory-many association

This method works the same for our third kind of many-to-many associations, the one that shows an optional-becoming-mandatory association. Try it for yourself, starting with this:

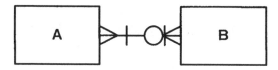

3.3 New notions

cardinality, optionality, degree, kind, nature

3.4 Exercise: Update the list of associations in your draft data map

1. Take the list of associations that you prepared in Section 2.11, and add the optionality indicators for each association, using the | character for

"mandatory," the o character for "optional," and |o for "optional-becoming-mandatory":

Association	Flavor
ARTWORK -|---|< IMAGE	P -|---|< P
IMAGE -|---o< IMAGE STRUCTURE	P -|---o< U
ARTWORK TYPE -|---|< ARTWORK	T -|---|< P
ARTWORK -|---o< REFERENCE	P -|---o< P
etc.	etc.

2. For each pair of entities, write the equivalent Business Statement:
   a) Each ARTWORK must be shown in one or more IMAGEs.
   b) Each IMAGE may have zero, one, or more IMAGE STRUCTUREs.
   c) Each ARTWORK TYPE must describe one or more ARTWORKs.[38]
   d) Each ARTWORK may be described in zero, one, or more REFERENCEs.
   e) etc.
3. Compare each of these Business Statements to the ones that you used in building your data map. Make revisions as necessary.
4. If you revise a Business Statement, go back to your associations list (step 1, above) and revise the association between the relevant entities.
5. If you revise an association, revise your data map.
6. Using your revised associations list as a guide, complete the table of primary and foreign keys that you started in Section 1.6.

4. VALIDATE ASSOCIATIONS ON THE DATA MAP

If you've been doing the exercises at the end of each step, you've probably been revising your data map. That's what happens when you think about things in more detail.

---

[38] Actually, we should map this as ARTWORK TYPE -|---o< ARTWORK: "Each ARTWORK TYPE may describe zero, one, or more ARTWORKs." After all, you will probably want to populate the list of artwork types first, then associate an artwork with an existing type when you enter it into your database. So we should define the association so that an ARTWORK TYPE can be unused (at least initially).

You're now in a position to test the associations on your data map. Below you'll find lists of valid, "red flag," and invalid associations. They're mostly concerned with one-to-one and one-to-many associations, since you have probably resolved all the many-to-many associations already. Check your own associations list against these lists, and make any changes you think are necessary. Then revise your data map (again).

For reference, we'll repeat the summary of the one-to-many relationships that are possible with various flavors of entities:

Flavor	Can be a Parent to	Can be a Child to
Principal (P)	P, R, S, U, I, T[1]	T, P, S
Intersecting (I)	I	P, S, I
Secondary (S)	S[2], P, R, U, I	T, P, S
Type (T)	R, P, S	P[1]
Role (R)	U	T, P, S
Structure (U)	None	P, S[3], R

[1] A dynamic principal entity cannot be a parent to a T entity. A static principal entity can be a parent to a T entity.

[2] A secondary entity that is parent to another secondary entity is in fact a mixed secondary/principal entity if both secondary entities descend (ultimately) from the same parent.

[3] A structure entity can be a child to a pure secondary entity or a mixed secondary/principal entity, but the association will probably be handled at the top level, in a dynamic-PU association.

4.1 Valid dynamic-P-to-dynamic-P associations

Here's our list of valid *dynamic-P-to-dynamic-P* associations:

P -|---o- P	P -|---o|< P
P -|---o|- P	P -|---|< P
P -|---o< P	---

Notice that one association is omitted:

$$P -|---|- P$$

If you run across an association like this, you've got a spot of trouble, because both ends of the association are the same, and the foreign key can't be determined. That's called an **equal association**. We'll get to that later.

4.2   Valid dynamic-P-to-S associations

Our list of valid *dynamic-P-to-S* associations is quite short:

$$P -|---o- S$$

That's the meaning of the "org chart" relationship between principal (supertype) and secondary (subtype) entities: "Each A may be one (and only one) B." For example, an artwork may be a painting or it may be a sculpture or any other type; but it can be only one painting or sculpture, etc. Of course, if the relationship isn't exclusive, if more than one subtype can apply to an instance of P, well, then we've got roles, and we'll use a role entity to straighten things out.

4.3   Valid dynamic-P-to-R associations

That said, we have only one valid association for dynamic-P-to-R:

$$P -|---|< R$$

For example, "Each EMPLOYEE must have one or more EMPLOYEE ROLEs." An employee cannot be an employee without a role, and that means that an employee cannot start without a role and then acquire one over time.

4.4   Valid dynamic-P-to-I associations

In its associations with dynamic P entities, an intersecting entity is always the child entity, and it always resolves a many-to-many association, so only one-to-many associations are valid for P-to-I. But all three flavors are valid:

| P -\|---\|< I | P -\|---o< I | P -\|---o\|< I |

4.5   Valid dynamic-P-to-U associations

Likewise, only one-to-many associations are valid for dynamic-P-to-U. And, as with an intersecting entity, all three flavors are valid:

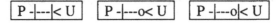

| P -\|---\|< U | P -\|---o< U | P -\|---o\|< U |

4.6   Valid T-to-P associations

A dynamic P is the child in a *T-to-dynamic-P* association, so we have three valid flavors:

| T -|---|< P | | T -|---o< P | | T -|---o|< P |

Actually, the first association is pretty much equivalent to the second. If every instance of T is used in P, T -|---|< P: all well and good. If not, well, you can easily define an instance of T (call it "type 0" [zero]) and give it the name of the P entity. Then, any instance of P that doesn't relate to a subtype can be designated "type 0". The effect is the same as defining the association as T -|---o< P. As a practical matter, you will probably want to use T -|---o|< P for most situations.

As for the "mandatory" on the P side (the first association above), think of it as a restriction: each type must have at least one instance of P associated with it. But it's common to create types in anticipation that something of that type will exist. For example, you create an art gallery that has only paintings in it. But you would define a type called SCULPTURE expecting that someday you will add a statue to the collection (the third association above). Declaring the association "optional" on the P side (the middle association above) lets a type category be empty if necessary.

4.7   Valid T-to-R associations

We get a similar situation with *T-to-R* associations. A role entity is always a child entity, so no one-to-one associations apply. All three one-to-many associations are valid:

| T -|---|< R *Unlikely* | | T -|---o< R | | T -|---o|< R |

The first of these associations is unlikely: a type isn't usually required to have an association with a role.

4.8   Valid R-to-U associations

A structure entity can be a child to a dynamic principal entity (in an exclusive type relationship) or to a role entity (in an inclusive type relationship). Only one-to-many associations are valid for *R-to-U*. As with an intersecting entity, all three flavors are valid:

| R -|---|< U | | R -|---o< U | | R -|---o|< U |

4.9 Valid static-P-to-any associations

A static principal can be parent to any flavor of entity, including another static principal entity (an unlikely prospect). It can also be a child to another static principal entity, but not to any other kind of entity. Only one-to-many associations are valid for *static-P-to-any* (where "any" = any other flavor of entity). The association is not identifying. All three flavors of one-to-many association are valid:

static P -|---|< any	static P -|---o< any	static P -|---o|< any

4.10 Red Flags

Let's look now at some "red flag" associations:

-|o---o-	-|o---o|<
-|o---o<	-o---o<

In each case, the relationship between the entities is unclear, because we don't have a strong "mandatory one" on one side. Now, in the first three we do have an optional-becoming-mandatory relationship defined on one side, and in the last case we have a parent defined. So we can say with reasonable certainty which table is going to be dependent (i. e., contain a foreign key).

What do you do if you have one of these connectors in your data map?

1. Go back to the original Business Statement and see if you've translated it correctly.
2. Try writing out the relationship in clear English (or whatever language suits you).
3. Go back to your subject matter expert and ask more questions.

You may be able to rewrite the association based on good evidence and reasoning.

Here are some more "red flag" associations:

---o<	---o|<
---o|-	---<
---o-	---|<

In each case, we're missing that strong "mandatory" on one side. As a result, we have associations that are essentially undefined (and therefore unimplementable in their current state). If you're mapping by hand, these connectors are usually transcription errors, pure and simple. But check them to be sure, and gather more information if necessary.

4.11 "Equal" associations

Here are some more "red flags":

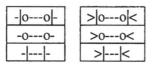

All of these are *equal associations*—the same on each end.

If we remember that entities are realized as tables, the problem with equal associations becomes clear. We don't know which table is going to contain information about the other. Will it be the left-hand one or the right-hand one? Worse, it might be both, and then we'd have information duplicated in or divided between two tables.

4.12 "Equal" many-to-many associations

Notice that the right-hand three associations in the list above are many-to-many associations. It's worth looking at them in a little more detail. Let's imagine two dynamic principal entities, X and Y, and an intersecting entity, XY:

1. X >|o---o|< Y resolves to X -|---o|< XY >|o---|- Y.
2. X >o---o< Y resolves to X -|---o< XY >o---|- Y.
3. X >|---|< Y resolves to X -|---|< XY >|---|- Y.

In each case, the dynamic-P-to-I association is valid.

Here are a few other many-to-many associations:

- X >|---o|< Y resolves to X -|---o|< XY >|---|- Y.
- X >o---o|< Y resolves to X -|---o|< XY >o---|- Y.
- X >o---|< Y resolves to X -|---|< XY >o---|- Y.

Again, in each case, when we resolve the many-to-many association into two one-to-many associations, the resulting associations are valid.

But what if we hadn't resolved these associations? Well, many-to-many associations just are not implementable in a relational database: you *have* to resolve them.

On the other hand, many-to-many associations *can* be implemented in object-oriented database systems. Check with your project manager or IT manager about the target system and the methods that will be used—but don't count on an object-oriented system to bail you out of a difficult analysis problem.

4.13 Optional-one-to-mandatory-many

Finally, let's look at the dog of the bunch:

$$X\text{ -o---}|<\text{ }Y$$

This is unimplementable. If we try to read it, we don't know whether we've got a *may* or a *must* relationship: it's saying one thing on one side of the sheet, and another thing on the other side. Solution: go back to the subject matter expert. There may be entities out there that have yet to be identified.

4.14 Valid Associations Summary: Dynamic P, I, T, R, S

Association	Comment
P -|---o- P	Ok
P -|---o|- P	Ok
P -|---o< P	Ok
P -|---o|< P	Ok
P -|---|< P	Ok
P -|---o- S	Ok
P -|---|< R	Ok
P -|---|< I	Ok
P -|---o< I	Ok
P -|---o|< I	Ok
P -|---|< U	Ok
P -|---o< U	Ok
P -|---o|< U	Ok
I -|---o- I	Unlikely
I -|---o|- I	Unlikely
I -|---o< I	Unlikely
I -|---o|<I	Unlikely
I -|---|< I	Unlikely
T -|---|< P	Ok
T -|---o< P	Ok
T -|---o|< P	Ok
T -|---|< R	Unlikely
T -|---o< R	Ok
T -|---o|< R	Ok

Association	Comment
R -|---|< U	Ok
R -|---o< U	Ok
R -|---o|< U	Ok
S -|---o< S	Ok

4.15 Valid Associations Summary: Static P

Association	Comment
static P -|---o< any	Ok
static P -|---o|< any	Ok
static P -|---|< any	Ok

4.16 "Red Flag" Associations Summary[39]

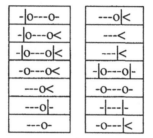

4.17 Exercise: Check your associations list for validity

1. Take the associations list that you updated in Section 3.4, above, and check each association against the valid associations given in the summary table above.
2. Note any associations that are indicated as "unlikely." Rethink them.
3. Check any remaining associations against the "Red Flag" associations listed in the table above. Rethink and revise.
4. As necessary, update the data map and the list of primary and foreign keys.

---

[39] Many-to-many associations are omitted because you should be able to resolve them.

Chapter 6

THE ART GALLERY WEB (CONTINUED)

Wherein Dr. Pangloss tries to get it right

"Next, [says Dr. Pangloss,] I turned to attributes. First, I associated attributes with entities based on the business rules. Then I identified primary keys."

9. Identify Attributes – draft

ARTWORK	title, creation date, accession number, classifiers (era, origin, period style, subject, affinity group), comment
ARTIST	name, pseudonym, active dates
IMAGE	filename
LOCATION	name, city, country
REFERENCE	author, book title, publication date, place of publication, publisher
PAINTING	same as ARTWORK
SCULPTURE	same as ARTWORK
ARCHITECTURE	same as ARTWORK
DECORATION	same as ARTWORK
OTHER	same as ARTWORK

"This list should have told me something immediately. Subtype entities are used for storing different data about different subtypes. If the attributes for PAINTING are the same as those for ARTWORK, then why have PAINTING as a distinct entity? If I were keeping information about media ('oil on panel' and the like), then PAINTING would have to have a 'media' entity. But I'm not.

"I got the message eventually."

10. Define Primary Keys for Principal Entities

ARTWORK	artwork no#
ARTIST	artist no#
IMAGE	filename#

LOCATION	location no#
REFERENCE	reference no#

"It was easy for me to decide that, except in the case of IMAGE, I would have to generate a serial number as the primary key for each principal entity. Names, whether of people, books, or works of art, are no good as unique identifiers, and what constitutes a LOCATION is a bit problematic. But an instance of IMAGE is uniquely identifed by its filename because the only kind of image we're using is an electronic file. Two different files can't have the same filename and be in the same space (folder/directory), and the files we're using are all in a few specific, well-controlled directories.

"In order to identify foreign keys, I had to take the next step and create the required meta-entities."

11. Second Draft Data Map

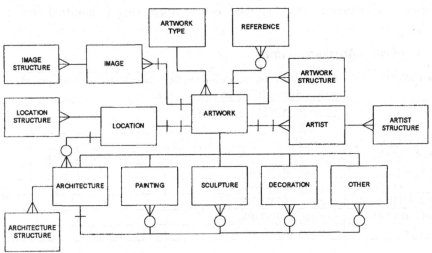

Added entities
- o *ARTWORK TYPE*
- o *IMAGE STRUCTURE*
- o *ARTIST STRUCTURE*
- o *ARTWORK STRUCTURE*
- o *LOCATION STRUCTURE*
- o *ARCHITECTURE STRUCTURE*

"From this draft, I derived the foreign keys."

12. Define Primary and Foreign Keys

ENTITY	Primary Key	Foreign Key
ARTWORK	artwork_no#	artwork_type_no#, location_no#
ARTIST	artist_no#	artwork_no#
IMAGE	filename#	artwork_no#
LOCATION	location_no#	
REFERENCE	reference number#	artwork_no#
PAINTING	artwork_no#	
SCULPTURE	artwork_no#	
ARCHITECTURE	artwork_no#	location_no#
DECORATION	artwork_no#	
OTHER	artwork_no#	
ARTWORK TYPE	artwork_type_no#	
IMAGE STRUCTURE	filename#, filename#	
ARTIST STRUCTURE	artist_no#, artist_no#	
ARTWORK STRUCTURE	artwork_no#, artwork_type_no#, artwork_no#, artwork_type_no#	
LOCATION STRUCTURE	location_no#, location_no#	
ARCHITECTURE STRUCTURE	artwork_no#, artwork_no#	
ARTWORK ARTIST	artwork_no#, artist_no#	

"I deleted the ARCHITECTURE STRUCTURE entity when I saw that every instance could be accommodated in the ARTWORK STRUCTURE entity. I added ARTWORK ARTIST when I realized I'd missed the many-to-many relationship between ARTWORK and ARTIST at the Business Statement level. Then I revised the data map again."

13. Third Draft Data Map

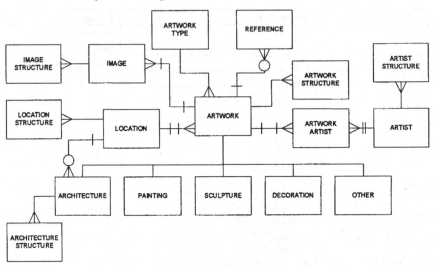

"Now I could create a more formal draft attribute list. I classified the attributes according to Mr. Finkelstein's types and wrote them according to his conventions.[40] Also, I added attributes that hadn't occurred to me when I wrote the business rules. And I chose names that would ensure that an attribute would exist in one and only one entity. I'm not worried about how long these names are: they'll change when they are translated into column names in the physical database."

14. Draft Entity List

ENTITY	primary key#	foreign key#	[selection attribute]	(group attribute)
ARTIST	artist_no#			(artist name, artist dates)
LOCATION	location_no#		[country, city]	
IMAGE	filename#	artwork_no#		
REFERENCE	reference_no#	artwork_no#	[reference author]	(reference title)

---

[40] Finkelstein 1992: 35-38. The various types of attributes are discussed in Chapter 7.

ENTITY	primary key#	foreign key#	[selection attribute]	(group attribute)
ARTWORK	artwork_no#	artwork_type_no#, location_no#	[genre, era, origin, period style, affinity group]	(artwork date)
ARCHITECTURE	artwork_no#	location_no#		
PAINTING	artwork_no#			
SCULPTURE	artwork_no#			
DECORATION	artwork_no#			
OTHER	artwork_no#			
ARTWORK ARTIST	artwork number#, artist number#			
ARTWORK TYPE	artwork_type_no#		[artwork type name]	
ARTWORK STRUCTURE	artwork_no#, artwork_type_no#	artwork_no#, artwork_type_no#		
ARTIST STRUCTURE	artist_no#	artist_no#		
LOCATION STRUCTURE	location_no#	location_no#		
IMAGE STRUCTURE	filename#	filename#		

ENTITY	((repeating group attribute))	{derived attribute}	other attributes
ARTIST			artist pseudonym, artist alphabetizer, artist active year
LOCATION			location name, location URL
IMAGE			copyright owner, image accession number, image focus, image comment
REFERENCE			
ARTWORK	((subject, artwork comment, citation))		artwork title, artwork accession number, artwork alphabetizer
ARCHITECTURE			
PAINTING			
SCULPTURE			
DECORATION			
OTHER			
ARTWORK ARTIST			artwork artist relationship
ARTWORK TYPE			

ENTITY	((repeating group attribute))	{derived attribute}	other attributes
ARTWORK STRUCTURE			artwork relationship
ARTIST STRUCTURE			artist relationship
LOCATION STRUCTURE			location relationship
IMAGE STRUCTURE			image relationship

"Perhaps I should have done this before, but I found it easier at this stage to write definitions for all the attributes. This exercise made me think more deeply and exposed further points for revision. As always, I noted my thinking as I encountered problems"

15. Attribute Definitions

Entity	Attribute	Definition	Examples
ARTIST	artist_no#	serial number	
ARTIST	(artist name)	name of artist: first name, last name	Paolo Caliari, Bonifacio de' Pitati, C. B. van Everdingen
ARTIST	(artist dates)	dates of artist's birth, death, activity, or florescence	1528 - 1588, ca. 1375 - 1444, act. 1475/1510
ARTIST	artist pseudonym	alternative name for artist; often the better known name	Veronese, Bonifacio Veronese
ARTIST	artist alphabetizer	term that will be used when alphabetizing the artist; usually part or all of the name or pseudonym	Veronese, Pitati, Everdingen
ARTIST	artist active year	number that will be used for constructing a timeline; usually the midpoint in the artist's life	1558, 1405, 1492
LOCATION	location_no#	serial number	
LOCATION	[country]	name of the nation in which the location resides	United Kingdom, Germany

Entity	Attribute	Definition	Examples
LOCATION	[city]	name of the city in which the location resides	London, Berlin-Dahlem
LOCATION	location name	name of the location	National Gallery, Gemäldegalerie Alte Meister, Lenbachhaus
LOCATION	location URL	URL of the location	http://www.land-sbg.gv.at/residenzgalerie/
IMAGE	filename#	name of the image file	aa003.jpg
IMAGE	copyright owner	owner of the copyright of the image; not currently used	
IMAGE	image accession number	number assigned by the copyright owner to the image; not currently used	
IMAGE	image focus	term indicating the relationship of the image to the artwork	detail
IMAGE	image comment	text describing the quality of the image	Note: The slides from the Tate and the Victoria and Albert have for the most part faded badly, and the image colors are unreliable.
REFERENCE	reference_no#	serial number	Consider replacing this with a standard citation form—for example, "Beck 1981."
REFERENCE	[reference author]	name of the author or authors of the reference work: first name, last name	Should be a group attribute or repeating-group attribute, not a selection attribute.
REFERENCE	(reference title)	title of the reference work	Should be broken out into title, publication information, and title structure, i. e., volume number, edition number, etc.
ARTWORK	artwork_no#	serial number	
ARTWORK	[genre]	descriptor for kind of content represented in or by the artwork	portrait, altar, historical, landscape Should be a repeating-group attribute.

Entity	Attribute	Definition	Examples
ARTWORK	[era]	name of the historical period associated with the artwork	Renaissance
ARTWORK	[origin]	name of the society or social group associated with the artwork	Benin, Apache Should be a repeating-group attribute.
ARTWORK	[period style]	name of the stylistic group associated with the artwork	Pre-Raphaelite, Baroque, Impressionism
ARTWORK	[affinity group]	name of the group of artists associated with the artwork	Pre-Raphaelites, Modern American Impressionists Should be moved to ARTIST or deleted.
ARTWORK	(artwork date)	date or dates of creation of the artwork	ca. 1638/40, 1611/12, ca. 1620/30? 1635/38?, after 1640, 1629 Obviously, an artwork date is composed of an optional modifier (ca., fl., etc.) and a year. This could be handled as two attributes.
ARTWORK	((subject))	content represented in the artwork	Madonna and Child, St Christopher
ARTWORK	((artwork comment))	textual commentary on the artwork	An unfinished portrait in the Dulwich Picture Gallery has been identified, doubtfully, as of the Duchess.
ARTWORK	((citation))	source and page numbers for the textual commentary on the artwork	Dejardin 138-39 The citation source is the foreign key relating the artwork to the reference. Error in Business Statement: should be ARTWORK>|---o<REFERENCE.
ARTWORK	artwork title	title of the artwork	The Four Philosophers
ARTWORK	artwork accession number	designator of the artwork in the museum holding it	1890 no. 1165
ARTWORK	artwork alphabetizer	term used for alphabetizing artworks in lists	Four Philosophers
ARTWORK ARTIST	artwork artist relationship	term describing any special relationship between the	attributed to, workshop of, follower of

Entity	Attribute	Definition	Examples
		artwork and the artist	
ARTWORK TYPE	[artwork type name]	type of artwork (usually indicates medium)	painting, sculpture, architecture, decoration, other Probably will be made attribute of ARTWORK.
ARTWORK STRUCTURE	artwork relationship	term describing relationship of artwork to artwork	contained in, part of
ARTIST STRUCTURE	artist relationship	term describing relationship between artist and artist	working with Possibly unnecessary: can be subsumed in ARTWORK ARTIST.
LOCATION STRUCTURE	location relationship	term describing relationship between location and location	contained in Possibly unnecessary: can be subsumed in ARTWORK STRUCTURE.
IMAGE STRUCTURE	image relationship	term describing relationship between image and image	thumbnail of Possibly unnecessary.

"As I drew the 4th draft data map, I made decisions based on my notes on the attribute definitions, and I revised the Entity-Entity Matrix and subsequent documentation. [Changes omitted from the text above.] Specifically, I decided:

- We weren't going to discuss artists apart from their art, and therefore we didn't really need ARTIST STRUCTURE. If an artwork was created by more than one artist, that would be shown in ARTWORK ARTIST, and so could relationships like 'workshop of' or 'follower of.'
- I retained LOCATION STRUCTURE to allow for named collections within museums, and I retained IMAGE STRUCTURE on the intuition that it would be at least as easy to associate an image with its thumbnail as it would be to create an ARTWORK IMAGE intersecting entity that would have two instances for every artwork.
- The case of a location being itself a work of art is rare, so it seemed reasonable to get rid of the association between LOCATION and ARCHITECTURE. This rare case could be handled by **denormalization**: by recording the same building in both LOCATION and ARTWORK.
- Deleting this association allowed me to delete all the subtypes and replace them with an 'artwork type' attribute in ARTWORK. I had

noticed that I'd omitted an important type (graphics) and likely had omitted others. More importantly, no special information needed to be stored relating only to a specific type.

- I'd discovered I'd missed part of the relationship between ARTWORK and REFERENCE: an artwork have comments from a number of references. Initially, I created an intersecting entity called ARTWORK REFERENCE. But when I looked at the new entity's compound primary key (<u>artwork no#</u>, <u>citation#</u>), I realized that it wasn't unique: an artwork might have more than one comment from the same reference.

- Also, I started thinking that if I defined 'comment' as a repeating-group attribute, I was going to burden the ARTWORK table with a lot of chunks of text. Maybe this is not a problem for a modern database, but I suspect it is. So I ditched ARTWORK REFERENCE in favor of COMMENT, which would have a serial number primary key, 'comment' and 'pages' as non-key attributes, and artwork_number# and citation# as foreign keys. (Actually, the entity name doesn't matter: it still provides the functionality of an intersecting entity, just with an originating primary key.)

"And so I produced the next revision."

16. Fourth Draft Data Map

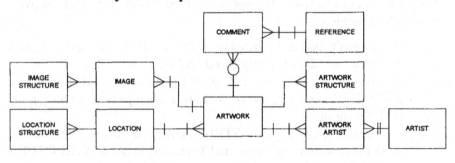

[To be continued ...]

Chapter 7

DEFINING ATTRIBUTES

Wherein we do a lot of detailing

As you approach the fatal threshold—talking with the database people—you have to develop more detailed information about the entities you've identified. We're talking about attributes.

Let's start by summarizing what we know:

- An attribute is a characteristic of an entity. More precisely, it is a defined category of meaningful information within the entity—like address-zipcode in the entity ADDRESS.
- Just as entities usually become tables in the database, attributes usually become columns in the table.
- Primary keys and foreign keys are attributes. (Non-key attributes are also attributes.)
- Standard Form VI lists an entity's attributes.
- Standard Form VII lists an attribute's properties.

It's not uncommon to mistake an attribute for an entity. For example, consider the secondary entities of ARTWORK: PAINTING, SCULPTURE, ARCHITECTURE, DECORATION, OTHER. If we're going to keep information about paintings that we don't keep about sculptures, such as medium and substrate ("oil on linen"), then PAINTING is an entity and painting-medium and painting-substrate are attributes of PAINTING.

But maybe we're going to record the materials that each artwork is made of. We could have artwork-material as one attribute of ARTWORK and artwork-genre as another. If PAINTING has no attributes other than primary or foreign keys, it isn't being used to store painting-specific information, and thus it's not an entity. Instead, maybe "painting" is a value of the attribute artwork-genre, along with "sculpture," "architecture," "drawing," and any others we like.

In sum, an entity defines the information that it will store about its instances. Within the entity, attributes identify the specific kinds of information that will be stored for those instances.

One thing about attributes makes them like entities: a particular attribute can exist only once in the properly normalized data model (except, of course, for foreign keys). Consequently, a particular attribute can exist in one and only one entity. That doesn't mean you can't have more than one date or comment or citation as an attribute in your data model. But the date an account was opened and the date a withdrawal was made are two different dates, represented by two different attributes.

It isn't always easy to say what attribute should be assigned to what entity. That's a matter for case-by-case analysis. But when it comes to principal and secondary entities, there is a general rule: assign the attribute to the highest-level (most general) entity for which it is meaningful. If an attribute applies to all instances of the parent entity, whatever their category, assign it to the parent. That's what we did with ARTWORK, artwork-material, and artwork-genre.

Now it's time to define attributes more fully, in terms that the Database Administrator can use. You'll need to

- distinguish different kinds of attributes
- define each attribute's properties completely.

One thing, though. You're doing *logical* data modeling, not *physical* data modeling. That means you'll be defining attributes from the business point of view. Let the database people define the specifics of implementation. We'll clarify this point a bit as we go forward.

1.   KINDS OF ATTRIBUTES

Here's the basic list:

- Primary key
- Foreign key
- Selection attribute
- Group attribute

- Repeating group attribute
- Derived attribute
- Non-key attribute (i. e., none of the above).

1.1 Primary key

A primary key uniquely identifies what will become a row in a table. It may be one **atomic** (i.e., indivisible) attribute or more than one: one column or more than one column. Whether atomic or not, the primary key may originate in the current entity, or it may be inherited, all or in part, from one or more parent entities. The inherited attributes are, of course, foreign keys in the child entity.

All components of the primary key have to be documented. If the component originates with the entity, say so. If it is inherited, well, keep reading.

1.2 Foreign key

A foreign key is an atomic attribute. For documentation purposes, you will need to record

- the entity where the key originated
- the intervening entities, if any, through which the key was copied down on its way to your child entity
- whether the foreign key is part of a compound primary key.

If the foreign key exists in a structure entity as part of the primary key, you will need to assign it an **alias** (such as *parent* or *child*, *superior* or *subordinate*). After all, a structure entity will have a two-part foreign key inherited from instances of the same parent entity. One part of the key will identify one instance, and the other will identify the related instance. The alias is the label that distinguishes between the two instances.

1.3 Selection attribute

A selection attribute (sometimes called a "secondary key") is an attribute or combination of attributes that can be used for searching through the instances of an entity and pulling out those that match. In physical database terms, it's something you may want to index.

Usually, choosing selection attributes is something that's done during physical data modeling, when the database people can weigh in with all the methods at their disposal. But if your users are going to get what they want, you have to think about selection attributes in business terms.

Consider the poor folks in Human Resources. They aren't always going to have the employee ID number (the primary key) available when they search the employee database. Instead, they'll search by last name, then select the right employee from a list of all employees having that same last name.

In fact, every principal or secondary entity that has an artificial primary key (like a student ID number or employee ID) is probably going to need a selection attribute. Artificial primary keys are good for ensuring that every instance is unique, but they aren't much good for browsing. It's inevitable that some attribute or combination of attributes will do better at specifying the real-world meaning of each instance.

Meta-entities have similar qualities. If the entity—say, a type entity—has an originating primary key, that key (type no#) is artificial, and there will be a name attribute (type-name). If the entity is going to hold other information, the name attribute makes a good selection attribute for accessing that information. A role or intersecting entity may likewise have a name attribute, even if it doesn't have an originating primary key.

Other attributes may also be useful as selection attributes. For example, you may want to know what museums exist in a particular country. The "country" attribute of the MUSEUM entity would be a convenient selection attribute.

During implementation, the database people will decide whether to build an index based on your selection attribute or whether, instead, to let searches be done on the fly. Your only concern should be to reflect the business reality: what your users search for, and how. As you work more closely with the database people, you'll become more sensitive to patterns of usage, and you'll be better able to define good selection attributes.

1.4 Group attribute

A group attribute is *not* an atomic attribute. Instead, it is a container for a set of atomic attributes. For example, employee-name might contain first name, middle name, last name, suffix (Sr., Jr., III, etc.), and so forth. In another country it might be broken down into a personal name, a prefix (bin, al-), father's name, another prefix, family name, and so forth. In yet another country, we might have a family name and a given name—like, for instance, Chiang Kai-Shek.

Code numbers often turn out to be group attributes, with different meaningful components in different positions. For example, Fischer Connectors structures some of their part numbers like this:[41]

Part Number Example	S 101 A004-2 /2.8				
Part Number Elements	S	101	A004	-2	/ 2.8
Description	Body Type	Series	Contact Configuration	Options	Indicates cable clamp is included

A group attribute is a certain kind of shorthand. It's used to keep attributes together that will be broken out during implementation and appear separately in the physical data model.

1.5 Repeating group attribute

Like a group attribute, a repeating group attribute (also known as a "repeating attribute," "repeating group," "multi-value attribute") is a container. But instead of containing different things, it contains a number of instances of the same thing.

For example, an artwork may have a number of subjects. For example, Raphael's *Terranuova Madonna* shows Mary, the Christ Child, two saints, and a landscape. So we could define artwork-subject as a repeating group attribute for the entity ARTWORK. ARTWORK would have instances like this:

artwork id#	artwork-name	artwork-subject
1	Terranuova Madonna	Mary, Christ Child, saint, landscape
2	Baptism of Christ	Christ, saint, angel, landscape
3	Allegory of Time and Love	Venus, Cupid, allegory

In documenting a repeating group attribute, you will have to define the minimum and maximum number of items that the attribute will contain. But

[41] Adapted from the Fischer Connectors website, http://www.fischerconnectors.com/order/order.htm#101. Code structures are discussed in detail in Burch and Grudnitski 1989: 193ff.

you needn't put too fine a point on it. Your repeating group attribute isn't long for this world, as you'll see when we consider normalization.

1.6 Derived attribute

A derived attribute is an attribute that is created from attributes of the same or other entities. Almost always, a derived attribute is the result of some calculation by formula or aggregation from multiple values of other attributes. Here are a few examples:

- date-hijri (date according to the Islamic calendar) is derived by formula from date-Gregorian or date-Julian, or vice versa
- days-elapsed is derived by subtracting date-start from date-current (or date-end, or whatever)
- requirement-value is derived by multiplying requirement-score by requirement-weight
- current-account-balance is probably derived by adding your bank account's month-end-account-balance to the aggregate of transactions (deposits and withdrawals) since end-of-month.

You may well ask: Why include a derived quantity in a database, when you can always calculate it? That's a question for the database people to answer. From the business side, your primary concern is to record it as an attribute and, if possible, define the formula for deriving it.

But there are a lot of calculations involved in business. Which ones do you represent as derived attributes?

Let's take date-hijri as an example. People in your business area make certain decisions based on the Gregorian date of a transaction. They make other decisions based on the Hijri date—say, a birth date or the commencement of an Islamic holiday. One date comes from one place, another from another. But time is time, and a day is a day, whatever the calendar.

The database people may decide that all dates will be calculated on the fly, whatever the calendar and purpose. They may decide, on the other hand, that it's cheaper to calculate once and store the result. That's their business, though, not yours.

Another example, closer to home. The month-end balance in your checking account is derived each month from the previous month's balance and the transactions during the month. It only makes sense to store that month-end balance, rather than recompute it each month starting from when you opened the account.

A derived attribute should never serve as a primary key. Other than that, it's like every other attribute: (1) a characteristic of an entity and (2) information that is worth storing.

One last note: because a derived attribute does depend on other attributes, it may pose problems for normalization. If the derived attribute can be placed in the same table as the attributes it depends on, you avoid those problems. But often that isn't possible. In the case of your checking account, for example, it's doubtful that transaction information would be stored in the same database table as month-end balance.

2. DEFINING ATTRIBUTE PROPERTIES

It may seem tedious, but it's necessary: you must eventually define every attribute in detail. We'll start with a list of the properties you'll need to define, then go back and discuss each one:[42]

- Name
- Description
- Kind of attribute
- Edit rules
- Domain
- Related planning statement(s)
- Other items like abbreviations and acronyms used in the organization (as necessary).

2.1 Name

The rules for naming attributes are pretty much the same as those for naming entities. The name is

- a singular (not plural) noun
- the term used in the business
- unique within the data model

---

[42] This situation is considered in more detail in Reingruber and Gregory 1994.

- NOT a reserved word[43].

You'll want to avoid special characters (~, @, &, and the like). Of course, the hash mark (#) has a particular meaning and use. Also, avoid particular names, like the names of organizations or systems: particulars are data, not kinds of data, and they are inclined to change. If your project organization has a naming convention, follow it. Often, database applications impose limitations on the length of an attribute name.

Of course, different departments may have different names for the same attribute. Since you're developing a single database, you'll have to develop a standard name for the attribute. And different departments may use the same name for different attributes. That means you'll have to develop a set of standard names. Since the names you choose may affect the user interface (data entry, reports, etc.), you may have to enter into negotiations with the departments.

2.2 Description

The database you're designing may well have a long life. That means that it will be maintained by people who weren't in on its design and development. The descriptions that you write will have to communicate clearly to those people.

This applies whether you're describing attributes or entities. Your description must be

- About what the attribute or entity is, not when, where, or how it's used
- Understandable on its own, independent of other definitions
- Expressed in terms that are clear to the business audience, with a minimum of technical language and acronyms.

What you want to communicate, in the end, is a complete account of the attribute or entity itself, why it's important to the business, and why it's in the data model.

---

[43] A word used for special purposes by your database application program and thus unavailable for other uses.

2.3   Kind of attribute

This is simple enough. What kind do you have? Choose one or (as necessary) more, and add additional information as required:

Primary key	Name the component attributes, if the key is compound. If the key, wholly or in part, is a foreign key, add documentation for the foreign key. Notation: <u>primary_key#</u>.[44]
Foreign key	Identify the key's parent entity or entities, starting with the originating entity or entities. Notation: foreign_key#.
Selection attribute	This is also known as a secondary key or an alternative access key. Where an attribute is not unique, such as employee last name, it can still be used to locate each employee with the same name. When physically implemented, this attribute might be indexed with a non-unique index (that is, duplicates are allowed): many Jacksons may, for example, be employees. Notation: [selection_attribute].
Group attribute	Name the component attributes. Notation: (group_attribute).
Repeating group attribute ↖	This is a non-key attribute appearing one or more times within an entity, such as (for example) the names of all of an employee's dependent children. Break this attribute out into another entity on the many side of a one-to-many association. Notation: ((repeating_group_attribute)).
Derived attribute	Give the formula, using the exact names of any other attributes involved. For each of those other attributes, give the name of the entity in which it resides. Give any conditions that affect the derivation. Notation: {derived_attribute}.
Non-key attribute	This is a fundamental data attribute. It is not a key, nor is it any kind of selection, group, repeating group, or derived attribute. Notation: non-key_attribute.

2.4   Edit rules

When you add an instance to an entity, you add some or all of the particular information about that instance. Later, you may or may not add more information, and you may or may not change the information you've already stored.

Edit rules govern the creation and updating of information in an attribute. There are four kinds:

---

[44] Notation for the kinds of attributes is defined in Finkelstein 1992: 35-38.

Add now and modify later	Information must be provided when the instance is created, but it can be changed later.
Add now, cannot modify later	Information must be provided when the instance is created. From then on it's locked in and cannot be changed.
Add later and modify later	Information may be provided when the instance is created, or it can be provided later. It can also be changed later.
Add later and cannot modify later	Information may be provided now or later. But once it's there, it's locked in.

Of course, adding and modifying can be done either by human beings (through a user interface) or by any number of automated systems.

As you define attributes, you'll need to define the edit rule that governs each one. Usually, this is easy:

- A primary key will usually be "Add now, cannot modify later." If you are using something that can change, like last name (a bad choice for a primary key), you will probably use a different edit rule. Your enterprise modeling tool may require that the edit rule for a primary key be "Add now, cannot modify later."
- A foreign key will be "Add now" so that its value will be added whenever an instance is added to the child physical table. As for "modify/cannot modify later," that depends on the key it was copied from. If that key cannot change, it and the child (foreign) key will be "cannot modify later." If the parent's primary key can change, then the child's foreign key must be "modify later". (In physical database design, these issues are handled under the heading of "referential integrity," which we'll discuss later on.)
- Derived attributes will usually be "Add later and modify later." A derived attribute depends on one or more other attributes. If you were to set it to "Add now," you'd have to make certain that the other attributes were already populated with values. But if you define it as "Add later," it can be created automatically when the other attributes are populated.

2.5 Domain

The domain of an attribute is the set of values that the attribute can take. Essentially, you define the domain in terms of

- the kind of data AND
- (sometimes) the length of the value or the range of values.

In common parlance, there are general domains, called "data types," and specific domains, called "enumerated domains." An enumerated domain is a specific, restricted set of static values. For example, the nucleotides in DNA constitute an enumerated domain with four values: adenine, guanine, thymine, cytosine.

When it comes to the details of domains, each database application is different. Oracle provides options that Microsoft Access doesn't, and vice versa. Names for these options differ too. You'll get into the details when you work with the database people. For now, it's important to provide enough of the right business information. Implementation decisions will come later.

Here are several commonly used kinds of general domain:

- Character string
- Number
- Binary object
- Date/Time
- Money
- Other.

And here are guidelines for their definition.

2.5.1 Character string

A character string has two general characteristics: it will be read, and it will probably not be used for calculation. Thus, a ZIP code may or may not be a character string depending on the situation: it is usually less a number, more a string of numerals. If a ZIP code were to be used for calculations (a situation we have trouble envisioning), it might profitably be defined as a number. Certain character strings may be of particular interest, like email addresses and URLs (web addresses). Many database management systems provide specifically for these and other special character strings.

To define a character string, you need to give the kind of character and the maximum length or range of lengths (in bytes, i.e. characters) of the string. Generally, if you state the language or language family of the string, that should be enough to indicate kind. These days, text is often implemented in Unicode.[45]

When you specify the length or range of a character string, you need to say whether the length is fixed or variable. A zip code is a fixed-length string, five or nine characters, assuming the dash between groups is omitted. A person's age will range from zero to, let's say, 120 and thus can be accommodated within a fixed length of three characters. Long passages of text, on the other hand, are of variable length.

If you are going to perform arithmetic on a field, do not define it as a character string. Define it as a number or as date/time.

2.5.2 Number

A number may or may not be read by human beings, but it may be used for calculation. To define a number, you have to define the base: base 2 (binary), base 8 (octal), base 10 (decimal), base 16 (hexadecimal), etc. After that, you need to say whether it is

- Decimal (that is, it has a decimal point) and how many places are required right of the decimal point *OR*
- Floating-point *OR*
- Integer.

Finally, you define the length of the number or the range of its values. If you can't give a precise maximum value, give a top limit for either the number itself or the number of characters needed to represent it.

When the database people get this information, they'll make decisions based not just on the size of the number and the required precision, but on storage requirements as well. For example, in DB2, the data type "Smallint" (small integer) can handle numbers from -32,768 base 10 to 32,767 base 10, requiring two bytes of storage for each number. The data type "Int" (integer) can handle considerably larger numbers (-2,147,483,648 base 10 to 2,147,483,647 base 10), but it requires four bytes of storage. Double the storage requirements again, and you're using "Bigint" for big integers:

---

[45] Unicode, the successor to ASCII, is a universal encoding system for all languages. If your database application program supports Unicode, you're home free. If you want more information, see www.unicode.org.

-9,223,372,036,854,775,808 base 10 to 9,223,372,036,854,775,807 base 10 (Baklarz *et. al.* 2000: 212-13). But—and it's worth saying again—these are physical considerations and the province of the database specialists.

2.5.3 Binary object

A binary object is a graphics, sound, or video file, though it may also be a text or hybrid-content file in a proprietary format, like a Microsoft Word document or PDF file. For all practical purposes, it is a string of bits.

There are two ways to use a binary object as an attribute:

* To store files of one and only one specific format
* To store files of different formats.

The difference is fairly simple: in the latter situation, you will need to use a second attribute to identify the file format.

In either case, when you document the binary object, you will need to identify the format or formats. Are all the items going to be JPEG files? Or MP3s? AVI files? Or will some be one, some another? If you expect to deliver these files on a web, you should probably give the MIME type or types.[46]

As for length or range, it's enough to give the size of the largest file that might be stored. Different database applications define binary objects with different size constraints: DB2 defines CLOB (character large object, maximum 32 KB text) and DBCLOB (double byte character large object, greater than 32 KB text), where two bytes can represent one character (Baklarz *et al.*2000: 216-217).

2.5.4 Date/Time

There are four varieties of date/time: date, time, date and time, and interval. This last, "interval," means a length of time. It indicates how often an event will occur or the time between events.

---

[46] MIME is the acronym for "multipart internet mail extensions." A MIME type expression gives the broad type of file—audio, image, video, and the like—and a subtype indicating the specific format: midi, mpeg, bmp, jpeg, quicktime, etc. For a directory, see http://www.iana.org/assignments/media-types/.

Date/time is often communicated with patterns called **edit masks**. For example, here are edit masks for dates as understood by DB2 (Baklarz *et al.* 2000: 219):[47]

Standard	Edit mask
International Standards Organization (ISO)	YYYY-MM-DD
IBM USA Standard	MM/DD/YYYY
IBM European Standard	DD.MM.YYYY
Japanese Industrial Standard	YYYY-MM-DD
Site Defined	"depends on database country code"

Here are guidelines and examples for describing a date/time attribute:

Date	• Indicate the calendar if necessary: Gregorian, Hijra, Julian. If no calendar is specified, assume Gregorian. • Give an edit mask if possible. • Give examples, especially if the name of the month is going to be written out or abbreviated.
Time	• Give an edit mask if possible: HH:MM:SS. • Indicate whether hours will be presented in 12-hour or 24-hour format. • Give precision to the nearest second, tenth of a second, hundredth of a second, millisecond, etc.
Date and time	An appropriate combination of the above. Indicate if this is a timestamp (the moment the event occurred, as measured by the system clock).
Interval	• Give precision to the nearest second, tenth of a second, hundredth of a second, millisecond, etc. • Give the range of values: 1 < interval < 120 days, 1ms < interval < 1000ms.

If a date/time attribute reflects a system event, like the date and time when a field is updated, you probably don't need to specify it in detail.

2.5.5 Money

Money is fairly simple to specify. You need to indicate the currency.[48] You need to give the precision, as long as it agrees with the currency. (U. S. dollars may be presented as whole dollars or as dollars and cents, but yen are always yen.) You can give a format mask or examples. And you need to give the range of values or the maximum amount that will be stored in an instance. If an amount can be negative, you need to document that, too.

---

[47] YYYY denotes the year, MM the month, and DD the day.

[48] If possible, use the ISO 4217 currency code: http://www.xe.com/iso4217.htm.

2.5.6 Other domains

Most DBMS (database management system) engines define specialized domains that are of interest primarily to programmers and database people, and some such programs permit user-defined domains. None of these is your problem. But if you use artificial keys, you may use a "system controlled" domain provided by the DBMS. Such a domain may be either sequential—the next integer in a sequence that began when the first instance (record) was added—or a random or sequential, but unique, sequence of numerals and/or characters.

2.6 Related planning statement

As part of your description, you may need to identify one or more specific planning statements that justify including the attribute in your data model. At the very least, such statements can be used with an enterprise modeling tool like Visible Advantage to provide traceability. For example, in this Statement-Attribute matrix generated by Visible Advantage, business statements are listed in the leftmost column, attributes serve as column headings across the top, and a checkmark at an intersection indicates a relationship:

Data Objects / Statements	accession number	artist active year	artist alphabetizer	artist date	artist descriptor	artist name	artist number
ARTIST ALPHABETICAL LISTING (Business Rule)			√				
ARTIST DATE STRUCTURE (Business Rule)		√		√			
ARTIST IDENTIFICATION (Business Rule)						√	
ARTIST RELATED TO ARTIST (Business Rule)							
ARTIST RELATED TO ARTWORK (Business Rule)							
ARTIST RELATED TO COMMENT (Business Rule)							
ARTIST TIMELINE (Business Rule)		√					

2.7   Other items

Some software engineering tools let you specify **abbreviations** and/or **acronyms**. These are usually of concern during implementation, not during development of the logical data model. If you do use an abbreviation or acronym to construct an entity or attribute name, document it.

Integrity constraints[49] are limitations on the value of an attribute in relation to other values of that attribute in other instances. There are two kinds: (1) unique and (2) optional.

"Unique" means that no two instances within an entity may have the same value for the specified attribute at the same time. Primary keys are unique by definition, but other attributes may also have this quality. These attributes are often identified as **candidate keys**—attributes that, singly or in combination, could be used as primary keys.

"Optional" means that an instance may have no value—i. e., a null value—for the attribute in question. This is the same as "Add later": if you don't add the value now, it remains null until you add it—which may be never. A note of warning, however: "optional" often indicates that you need to look for secondary entities. If you don't do the work now, you may have to do it when you get to normalization.

Conversely, if an attribute is *not* optional, it must have a value for every instance within the entity. Different instances may have the same value for that attribute, or they may all have unique values. "Not optional" (also known as "not null") equates to the edit rule "Add now."

Keep your eye on optional attributes. We'll consider them again when we discuss normalization.

Some development or modeling methodologies require you to identify a **data custodian** and/or **data steward** for each entity and attribute. Definitions vary, but generally the data custodian makes policy for business information, including security and backup/storage. The data steward makes technical and operational decisions regarding storage, retrieval, processing, and data integrity. In a less formal setting, you may want to record the name

---

[49] Not the same thing as referential integrity.

or title of the person in the functional area who is responsible for the accuracy of the information.

3. NEW NOTIONS

atomic attribute, alias, selection attribute, group attribute, repeating group attribute, derived attribute, non-key attribute, edit rule, domain, binary object, edit mask, system-controlled, integrity constraint, candidate key, unique, optional, data custodian, data steward

4. EXERCISE: DOCUMENT YOUR ENTITIES AND ATTRIBUTES

Many shops don't bother to keep track of entities and attributes at this level, at least not manually. Such documentation is more easily done in an enterprise modeling tool. Nonetheless, these forms are useful as checklists. Adapt them as needed.

ENTITY NAME:	
Description:	
Flavor (circle 1) P / S / I / T / R / U	
Primary_key#	
Foreign_key#	Originating entity:
Foreign_key#	Originating entity:
Foreign_key#	Originating entity:
Other attributes:	
Abbreviations/Acronyms:	
Associated entities:	
Planning statement(s):	
Data Custodian/Steward:	

ATTRIBUTE NAME:			
Description:			
Resides in (entity name):			
Kind (circle 1 and complete associated documentation)			
Primary_key#	Originating? Y / N	Components (if foreign key, document below):	
Foreign_key#	Part of primary key? Y / N	Originating entities:	Alias:
Foreign_key#	Part of primary key? Y / N	Originating entities:	Alias:
[Selection_attribute]			
(Group_attribute)		Components:	
((Repeating_group_attribute))		Minimum occurrences:	Maximum occurrences:
{Derived_attribute}	Formula:	Related attributes:	Conditions:
Non-key_attribute			
Unique/candidate key? Y / N			
Edit rule (circle 1 in each column)	Add now (="not null") / Add later (="optional")	Modify later / Can't modify later	
Domain (circle 1 and complete associated documentation)			
Character	Language(s):	Fixed length / Variable length	Range / max length:
Number	Base:	Dec / FP / Int If decimal, give no. of places:	Range / max length:
Binary	File type(s):		Max file size:
Date / Time / Interval (circle)	Calendar:	Edit mask / example:	Precision (time): Range (interval):
Money	Currency: Can be neg? Y / N	Edit mask / Example:	Precision: Range / max length:
Other	Autonumber / Sys gen id		
Abbreviations/Acronyms:			
Planning statement(s):			
Data Custodian/Steward:			

Chapter 8

THE ART GALLERY WEB (CONTINUED)

Wherein Dr. Pangloss poses as a software engineer

"The next step [said Dr. Pangloss] was to load all my knowledge about the art gallery web into Visible Advantage and see what would happen."

17. Create planning statements in Visible Advantage

"After creating an encyclopedia (repository) for the project, I began entering planning statements—specifically, the business rules I'd identified. This gave me a chance to apply my improved understanding of the facts and to express them in more precise language than I had originally used. I recast certain planning statements (those for which a Standard Form exists) as explicit Business Statements, capitalizing nouns. Here's a sample:

Statement: ARTIST RELATED TO ARTIST

Text: Each ARTIST may collaborate with zero, one, or many other ARTISTs. One or more unnamed artists may be identified as the "follower(s)" of or as belonging to the "school" of or as comprising the "workshop" of a named artist.

Statement: ARTWORK RELATED TO ARTWORK

Text: Each ARTWORK may be part of another ARTWORK, either as a detail view or as a component.

Statement: ARTIST RELATED TO COMMENT

Text: Each ARTIST may be the subject of zero, one, or many COMMENTs. Each COMMENT may describe zero, one, or many ARTISTs.

Statement: COMMENT RELATED TO REFERENCE

Text: Each COMMENT has zero, one, or many CITATIONs. A comment that has no citation is assumed to originate with the owner of the art gallery web. A citation comprises a link to a reference work and, optionally, a page reference. The page reference may be one or more page numbers or ranges of page numbers. It may include a volume number or part and section numbers. It may include suffixes like "n" (footnote), "ff" (following), passim, or "n. 1" (note 1).

Statement: IMAGE IDENTIFICATION

Text: Each IMAGE is identified by its FILENAME. It may be described in terms of focus ("detail"), relative size ("thumbnail"), and visual quality. It may also have a copyright holder and an accession number in the copyright holder's inventory system.

Statement: IMAGE RELATED TO IMAGE QUALITY

Text: Each IMAGE may have zero, one, or many COMMENTs regarding image quality. These comments are often the same for a number of images. Each COMMENT may describe zero, one, or many IMAGEs. These comments never have a cited source. They may include the URL of an image collection on the World Wide Web.

Statement: LOCATION IDENTIFICATION

Text: Each LOCATION is identified by name, city, and country. It may also be identified by its inclusion in another location. Each LOCATION may have zero, one, or many WEBSITEs (URLs).

Statement: LOCATION RELATED TO LOCATION

Text: Each LOCATION may be part of another LOCATION, either physically (Chapel of Eleanora di Toledo, Palazzo Vecchio) or conceptually (Paul Mellon Collection, National Gallery of Art, Washington).

Statement: REFERENCE IDENTIFICATION

Text: Each REFERENCE is identified by the last name of its author or major authors, its date of publication, and an optional sequence letter (a, b, c).

Statement: REFERENCE RELATED TO COMMENT

Text: Each REFERENCE may provide zero, one, or many COMMENTs.

"At this point, I added ARTIST RELATED TO COMMENT and IMAGE RELATED TO IMAGE QUALITY. I'd realized that I had included some comments about artists, and they should be accommodated. Also, I decided to create an entity called IMAGE QUALITY to handle the comments I sometimes have to make about faded slides. I considered linking

IMAGE to COMMENT. But COMMENT is used to store text that is seldom reused, whereas comments on image quality are often repeated from image to image.

"In inputting the planning statements, I separated Business Statements (rules relating entities) from rules describing attributes.[50] I avoided writing business rules in terms of many-to-many associations. I'd already done the work to reduce those to one-to-many associations, and I saw no point in going backward. I tried to name the statements carefully, and I went to the trouble of editing the names for consistency.

"I printed out the Statement report and matched the rules against my updated Entity-Entity Matrix. As a result, I found seven or eight rules that I'd omitted. Most of them stated associations from 'the other direction'— from the point of view of the second of two associated entities.

18. Add entities and attributes in Visible Advantage

"I did the easy stuff first. Referring to the Statement report, I entered the five principal entities (ARTIST, ARTWORK, IMAGE, LOCATION, and REFERENCE) and the one intersecting entity (COMMENT). Then I went back and entered all the attributes that were simple to define, checking them off the report as I went.

"As I reviewed my notes, I edited the planning statements to describe attributes that I'd overlooked. Then I added the attributes to the entities. I did all this without, at this point, defining a link in VA between specific planning statements and specific entities or attributes.

"For ARTIST, ARTWORK, LOCATION, and IMAGE QUALITY, I defined a system controlled primary key. For IMAGE, the primary key is the name of the image file. I gave REFERENCE a good deal of thought and decided to do a little library research on the current preferred documentation style in art history.

19. Linking attributes to planning statements in Visible Advantage

"I wasn't yet ready to create associations and meta-entities, so I just linked planning statements to attributes for the entities I'd already input. After printing out the Statement-Data Matrix, I identified attributes that were

---

[50] Dr. Pangloss was using the Educational Edition of Visible Advantage, which has limits on the number of planning statements that can be defined.

not linked. A few were functional, so I went back and added planning statements, then linked them to the attributes. I decided that system controlled IDs didn't require planning statements.

"My biggest concern was the attributes that I hadn't yet defined—things like artist date, artwork date, the minor artwork descriptors, and the attributes of REFERENCE. I'd set them aside for the moment, and I just didn't want to forget them.

20. Defining associations in Visible Advantage

"Before defining associations in VA, I revised the data map to be as up-to-date and explicit as possible:

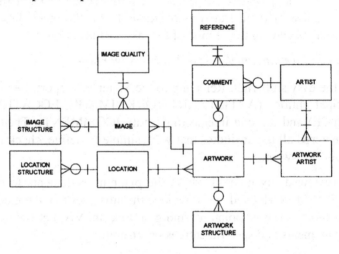

"Then I started entering the associations in VA. Of the entities I'd already entered, all but one was a principal entity. So I defined all the PP associations first, starting each time with the parent entity. Then I defined the meta-entities and their associations. I added key and non-key attributes and corrected the errors exposed by the Model Analysis report.

Solving a problem

"When I got to these associations—

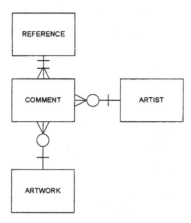

—I ran into a problem. I'd defined COMMENT in VA as an intersecting entity, so VA wanted an identifying association between ARTWORK and COMMENT. I had my doubts. On the other hand, I liked the idea of an identifying association between REFERENCE and COMMENT, because I wanted to use a short-form citation as REFERENCE's primary key.

"Thus, a dilemma. It's not good practice to go 'identifying' with the one parent and 'non-identifying' with the other. At first, I thought I'd go 'non-identifying' with both: create a system controlled ID for COMMENT, and bring in the parents' primary keys as foreign keys.

"Then I changed my mind. Instead of giving COMMENT a system controlled ID, I'd give REFERENCE one. The website's application program—whatever it might be—could grab the short-form citation from REFERENCE based on the information in COMMENT. In other words, it's a display issue, not a database issue.

"Just about this time, I realized that COMMENT isn't an intersecting entity, but a principal entity, with a three-part compound primary key: artwork_no#, artist_no#, reference_no#. This got me to thinking:

1. "Can either artwork_no# or artist_no# be left blank? Generally, we want to comment about an artwork or an artist, but not about both.
2. "What if the same text is relevant to more than one artist? Or more than one artwork? I don't want to be repeating long passages of text in the database.

"So I experimented. Perhaps COMMENT could be a parent to both ARTIST and ARTWORK. The associations would be non-identifying. COMMENT'S primary key would copy down to each of the other two entities. The changed part of the map looked like this.

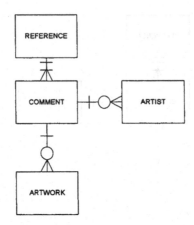

I made these changes in VA and ran the Model Analysis report to verify that everything was okay.

"These weren't the only questions I came up with, and it wasn't the end of my revisions to the data map. Every time I made a change, I ran the Model Analysis report, and that helped me stay on course."

[*And here we leave Dr. Pangloss. When he finally decides to migrate the web to the Internet, he'll follow the guidelines in Chapter 12, below: run a final, thorough check of the logical data model, then work on developing the physical database. And he'll start developing the applications that will draw on that database to generate pages for the Art Gallery website.*]

Chapter 9

VERIFYING THE DATA MODEL

Wherein we get it right

We're closing in on the Holy Grail: normalization and the end of things as we know them. But first you need to make one last check of the data model. We'll assume that

- All associations are one-to-one or one-to-many.
- All associations are valid.
- All primary and foreign keys have been determined for all entities.
- As many attributes as possible have been identified, documented, and assigned to the appropriate entities.

That done, you're in a good position to search for problem patterns:

- entity cycles
- triads
- multiple associations
- parallel intersecting entities
- one-to-one associations.

1. ENTITY CYCLES

You know what an **entity cycle** is:

- You can't get the job unless you have the experience. You can't get the experience unless you get the job.
- Your phone bill is out of order. You call the phone company and get the touch-tone menu. You press the right button, which gives you

another menu. You press the right button, which gives you another menu. You press the right button, and you're back at the original menu.

In sum, an entity cycle works like this: entity A depends on entity B, which depends on entity C, which depends on entity A. Add entities at your leisure: you always end up going in circles. In data modeling terms, no entity in an entity cycle is purely a parent entity, and all entities in an entity cycle are child entities.

1.1 Discovering entity cycles

The process for discovering entity cycles is direct and systematic. You start with a parent entity: an entity that is at the strong mandatory "one" end of an association. Then you follow the trail of associations, parent to child, parent to child, until—if you have an entity cycle—you end up where you started.

If you like a more formal set of instructions, here they are. Looking at your data map,

1. Identify groups of entities (a minimum of three per group) that are connected one to another.
2. Within each group, identify all possible closed paths (circles).
3. For each circle,
   a) Find a strong mandatory "one" (SM1) on one entity, and mark it as your starting point.
   b) Follow that association to the next entity.
   c) Find a SM1 on that entity, and mark it. OR If you find no SM1, proceed to step 3e below.
   d) Repeat from step 3b until you arrive at the entity where you started. Congratulations! You have identified an entity cycle. Mark it for later study.
   e) Repeat process (step 3) with the next circle.
4. Repeat process (from step 2) for the next group (to end).

And if you like to work from diagrams and examples:

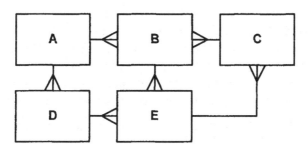

Here's a group of associated entities. You can break this group down into three circles:

- The outer circle, ABCED (= ADECB, DECBA, ECBAD, CBADE)
- The left-hand circle, ABED (= ADEB, BEDA, DEBA)
- The right-hand circle, BEC (= ECB, CBE).

Let's start with the outer circle, ABCED: A is parent to B, but B is not parent to C. The circle fails at entity B: no entity cycle. If you start at any other entity in the circle, you'll eventually end up stymied at entity B, without having found any entity cycles.

Now the left-hand circle, ABED: A is parent to B, B is parent to E, but E isn't parent to D. No entity cycle, no problem.

Finally, let's look at the right-hand circle, BEC: B is parent to E, E is parent to C, and C is parent to B. We have an entity cycle here.

So what's the problem? Well, an instance of E will be drawing on information contained in an instance of B (as indicated by the foreign key copied down from B). An instance of C will draw on information contained in that instance of E. And an instance of B will draw on information contained in that instance of C. Sure, this last instance of B may not be the same as the one E drew on. But HOW DO YOU KNOW? If you don't have a circle, you have a spiral of undetermined length. How will you process information like that? What we've got, folks, is an unimplementable mess.

1.2 Correcting entity cycles

As you should have realized by now, entity cycles are bad. They indicate

- An error in your data map *OR*
- Incomplete analysis *OR*
- A problem with your company's business processes.

Fortunately, the solutions are simple:

- Correct the error. Often the problem is that the cardinality is reversed: one-to-many when it should have been many-to-one. *OR*
- Go back and talk to the subject matter experts, rethink that portion of the data map, and make the necessary changes. *OR*
- Talk to the owners of the business processes and negotiate changes that will get rid of the entity cycle without creating new problems.

Often, you will find that you simply need to add an additional entity. See? We said it was simple.

2.   TRIADS

Now you're going to concentrate on groups of three entities connected in a circle. You've already weeded out the entity cycles among them. The ones that are left are called **triads**. A triad consists of exactly three entities having more than one path of associations between the highest level parent entity and the lowest level child entity. The usual solution to a triad is to remove the shorter path between the highest level parent entity and the lowest level child entity. For example, if

A ---< B, B ---< C, and A ---< C,

then simply removing A ---< C usually solves the problem. But as we will show, this solution does not work every time.

Here are eleven combinations of entity flavors that could qualify as triads:

- PIP, PPP, PPS, PSS, PII. See below.
- PPR. Of course, this case would never occur. A role entity can't be associated with more than one principal entity.
- PPT. This too would never occur. A type entity can't be associated with more than one principal entity.
- PPU. Nor can a structure entity be associated with more than one principal entity.
- PSU. The SU association isn't even a good idea in the first place. That aside, a secondary entity is a subset of a principal entity, so the triad boils down to PPU (invalid).
- PRT. This pattern would never occur. If we've got the role entity sitting between principal and type entities, we've got no reason to link T to P directly.

- PTU. This pattern would never occur. Where the U entity needs to include the value of P's key (for both the parent instance of P and the child instance of P), make the association from T to P identifying. The value of T's key will copy from T to P, and from P to U. It will also copy from P to all S entities.

That leaves five triads that are eager to give you problems. Let's look at each in turn.

2.1 PIP

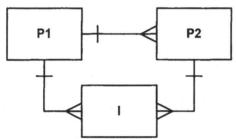

This is the easy one. The intersecting entity exists to resolve a many-to-many association between the two principal entities. So why do we need the one-to-many association from P1 to P2?

This triad probably came from where most triads come from: two or more Business Statements, usually from different areas of the enterprise, have been mapped concurrently. For example:

1. Each TEACHER (P1) has one or more COURSEs (P2).
2. Each COURSE (P2) has one or more TEACHERs (P1).
3. Each TEACHER (P1) may attend zero, one, or many COURSEs (P2).

The first two statements are from a staffing point of view; they establish a many-to-many association between the principal entities TEACHER and COURSE, and this many-to-many association is resolved by creating the intersecting entity. The third statement is from a "client" point of view. It establishes a one-to-(optional)-many association between the same two entities.

The resulting triad can't be resolved in isolation. We're going to have to look at attendance policies, employee classifications, employee benefits, and employee training requirements. Most likely, teachers aren't the only staff who may attend courses, and their attendance probably has nothing to do with which teachers teach which courses. One solution might be to add an attribute to the I entity describing the nature of the association, such as "teaches" or "takes" (a course).

2.2   PPP

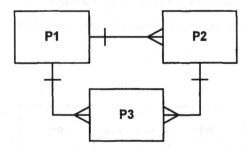

This triad generally reflects the concurrent mapping of Business Statements at two different levels of detail. For example:

1. Each DEPARTMENT (P1) markets one or many PRODUCT LINEs (P2).
2. Each PRODUCT LINE (P2) has one or many PRODUCTs (P3).
3. Each DEPARTMENT (P1) sells one or many PRODUCTs (P3).

The third Business Statement either gets to the point more quickly (maybe product_line is an attribute of PRODUCT) or bypasses a significant area of information. Perhaps product lines should be conceived as categories of PRODUCT. As with the PIP example, we need to think more deeply and gather more information. One solution might use three separate P entities for PRODUCT, PRODUCT LINE, and DEPARTMENT, with an I entity copying down a three part primary key for each valid combination.

2.3   PPS

In the PPS triad, two principal entities are associated with each other, and each is associated with a secondary entity. If that secondary entity is a subtype (a subset) of yet a third principal entity, well, the situation is functionally the same as with the PPP triad, so we can treat it as a PPP triad. If, on the other hand, S is a subtype of one of our two principal entities, then there are three cases, as follows:

2.3.1 Case 1 (Many-to-Many)

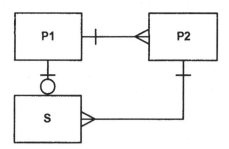

Here, P1 has a subtype; it has a one-to-many association with another principal entity, P2; and P2 has its own one-to-many association with the subtype. But S is a subset of P1. Therefore, we have the actual relationship between P1 and P2 is many-to-many. The obvious solution, then, is to ditch the association between S and P2 and create an intersecting entity between P1 and P2, like so:

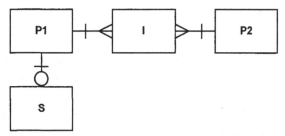

It may not be quite so simple, however. For example:

1. Each PERSON (P1) may be zero or one PILGRIM (S).
2. Each PERSON (P1) may have zero, one, or many BOTTLEs of water (P2).
3. Each BOTTLE of water (P2) may serve one or many PILGRIMs (P1).

The first of these Business Statements defines the association between P1 and S. The second defines the association between P1 and P2, and the third the association between P2 and S.

Notice, however, that the relationships in Business Statements 2 and 3 are different. Statement 2 is about possession or ownership. Statement 3 is about consumption. Furthermore, while the owner of a bottle of water may or may not be a pilgrim, the consumer is always a pilgrim. What we've got, then, is not just types (pilgrim or non-pilgrim) but roles (owner, consumer), and that fact has to be built into our data map. Again, one solution might be to add an attribute to the I entity describing the nature of the association, such as "owns" or "takes a drink from."

2.3.2 Case 2 (Many-to-One)

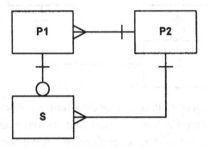

Again, P1 has a subtype, S. But its association with P2 is many-to-one. P2 has a one-to-many association with S, as before. But that association is covered in its association with P1. The association between P2 and S is redundant and can be ditched.

For example:

1. Each EMPLOYEE (P1) may be zero or one WELLDIGGER (S).
2. Each WAREHOUSE (P2) issues tools to one or many EMPLOYEEs (P1).
3. Each WAREHOUSE (P2) issues tools to zero, one, or many WELLDIGGERs (S).

A warehouse has to issue tools to at least one employee. That employee may or may not be a welldigger. But any employee who is issued tools— welldigger or not—will have that fact recorded in the EMPLOYEE table via the foreign key copied down from WAREHOUSE.

2.3.3 Case 3 (One-to-Many)

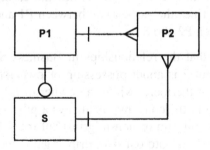

As before, P1 has a subtype, S. But P1's association with P2 is one-to-many, and so is S's association with P2. The latter association, between S and P2, is redundant and can be ditched—unless, of course, the two associations are reflecting different kinds of relationships. In that case, we have to think again—as usual. Note that this is an exception to our rule that a triad should be resolved by deleting the shorter association between the highest level parent and the lowest level child.

2.4 PSS

With the PSS triad, we're confronted with three general cases:

1. Both secondary entities are subtypes of the principal entity.
2. Only one of the secondary entities is a subtype of the principal entity.
3. Neither secondary entity is a subtype of the principal entity.

Actually, if you map out this third case, you'll see that it's actually two triads: one is our Case 1 or Case 2 (below), and the other is functionally equivalent to a PPP triad. We'll leave it for you to play with.

2.4.1 Case 1 (Subtypes of the Same Principal Entity)

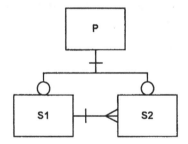

Here, P has two subtypes, S1 and S2. An instance of one S1 has an association with one or more instances of S2. If we look at the keys, we see that each S receives a copy of P's primary key, but S2 receives two: one copy from P (its primary key) and another copy from S1, as a foreign key.

The two keys in S2 should tell us that the real situation is recursion: instances of P relate to other instances of P. So, in addition to the type entity (not shown above), we're going to need a structure entity to sort things out. We may also need a role entity.

2.4.2 Case 2 (Subtypes of Different Principal Entities)

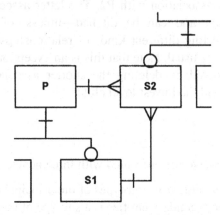

This diagram shows one of two versions of the case. Here, P and S1 both have a one-to-many association with S2. In the other version, these two associations are reversed in direction: S2 has a one-to many association with P and with S1. No matter: either way, the association between S1 and S2 is redundant and can be ditched. Another solution might be to associate P with S2's parent and delete the associations shown here between P and S2 and S1 and S2. Once again, we have found an exception to the rule that a triad should be resolved by deleting the shorter association between the highest level parent and the lowest level child.

2.5   PII

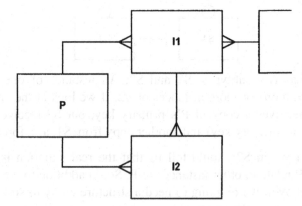

The problem with this triad becomes apparent when we look at the key situation. I1 has a compound primary key, and part of that key is the foreign key inherited from P. I2 likewise has a compound primary key, with one part inherited from P, the other from I1. But because P's primary key is part of I1's primary key, I2 ends up with two identical copies of P's primary key in its own primary key. But only one copy of P's primary key is necessary to establish the uniqueness of I2's primary key.

The obvious solution is to ditch the association between P and I2. A better solution is to think about how this triad came about in the first place.

3.   MULTIPLE ASSOCIATIONS

Now that we've got all entity cycles and triads straightened out, we need to look at associations between two entities. The basic rule is this:

- Two entities, one logical association: good.
- Two entities, more than one logical association: bad (mostly).

Let's look at some abstract patterns:

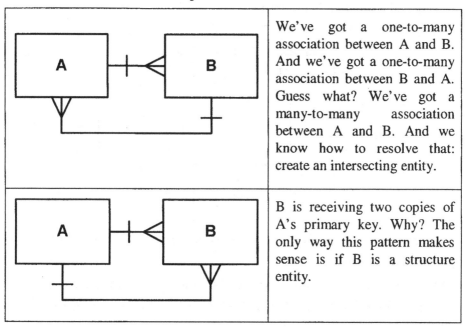

(diagram: A and B with two one-to-many associations)	We've got a one-to-many association between A and B. And we've got a one-to-many association between B and A. Guess what? We've got a many-to-many association between A and B. And we know how to resolve that: create an intersecting entity.
(diagram: A and B)	B is receiving two copies of A's primary key. Why? The only way this pattern makes sense is if B is a structure entity.

Of course, you might find three or more associations between the same two entities. But, however many associations there are, the reasons are the same: you've probably got conflicting Business Statements—perhaps subtypes that haven't been broken out into secondary entities. In theoretical terms, you probably haven't normalized to Third normal form.

4.   PARALLEL INTERSECTING ENTITIES

Finally, let's look at this multiple association:

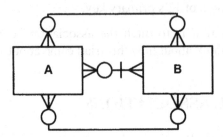

Well, this situation just shouldn't exist at all. We should have three intersecting entities resolving these many-to-many associations.

Or should we? Fact is, each intersecting entity on your data map should link a unique pair of principal entities.

Here's the situation in the abstract:

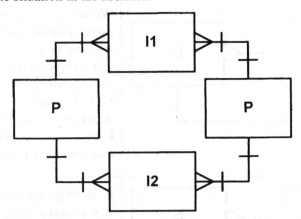

I1 has the same primary key as I2: pk1#, pk2#. Which entity do we go to to get the data we want?

By now you know why problems like this occur: you have multiple Business Statements, representing partial or conflicting views of the business situation.

Organizationally, the solution is the same as always: more analysis, more talking with the subject matter experts, maybe some talks with management. At the mapping level, the solution is usually quite simple: the parallel intersecting entities all collapse into one entity.

Or so we like to think. Imagine, for example, that you and a colleague have been working on the data model for Zachman Pie Company. You yourself have been working with the Product Development team, and you've come up with the following Business Statements:

1. Each PRODUCT has one or many INGREDIENTs.
2. Each INGREDIENT has zero, one, or many SUPPLIERs.
3. Each SUPPLIER supplies zero, one, or many INGREDIENTs.

You've mapped these Business Statements this way:

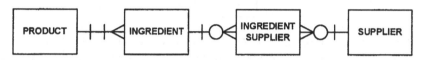

Since INGREDIENT and SUPPLIER have a many-to-many association, you've created the intersecting entity INGREDIENT SUPPLIER.

In comes your colleague. She's been talking to the folks in Purchasing, and she's come up with this mapping:

This seems quite reasonable, and she's got the Business Statements to prove it:

1. Each PRODUCT has zero, one, or many SUPPLIERs.
2. Each SUPPLIER supplies zero, one, or many PRODUCTs.

Nonetheless, it bothers you. And when you put the maps together, you like it even less:[51]

---

[51] This is not properly a diagram of parallel intersecting entities. Reality is sometimes messy.

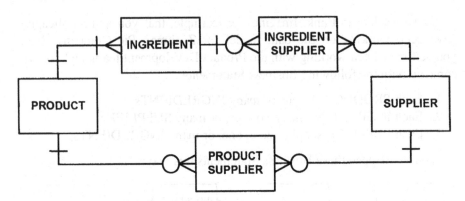

But your colleague takes one look and comes up with an answer: INGREDIENT is just a subcategory of PRODUCT. Her product list proves it: flour, sugar, sodium citrate, cardboard boxes, etc. Her revised data map looks like this:

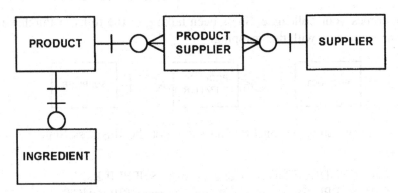

INGREDIENT SUPPLIER has disappeared from the map: it's been collapsed into PRODUCT SUPPLIER. No parallel intersecting entities, no triads: everything's in good form.

You don't buy it. Your product list includes pies, turnovers, and tarts. Ingredients aren't a subcategory. They're, well, ingredients. Besides, those pies, turnovers, and tarts come from Zachman, not from Pillsbury or International Paper.

Conclusion: PRODUCT means different things in different departments. To Product Development, it's what they develop for the company to manufacture. To Purchasing, it's what somebody else makes and the company buys. You're going to have to do a bit of work to come up with terms that both departments will accept, but once that's done, the map can be redrawn properly.

5.   ONE-TO-ONE ASSOCIATIONS

A scan of the Valid Associations Summaries (Chapter 5, secs. 4.14-4.15) tells us that there are only three valid one-to-one associations:

- Dynamic P -|---o- dynamic P
- Dynamic P -|---o|- dynamic P
- Dynamic P -|---o- S

We know this last one. It's the association between a supertype and one of its subtypes. We can set it aside. But the two P-to-P associations deserve a look.

Generally, if you've got a one-to-one association, you should be wondering why. Why isn't the child entity part of the parent entity? Why haven't the child's attributes been absorbed into the parent?

Often such situations arise from different modeling sessions or different business areas. Working with one group of subject matter experts, you created one entity. Working with another, you created another. The relationship is simple, but the information hasn't been integrated.

Note, however, that those two valid PP associations are one-to-optional-one. That means that for some instances of the parent entity there are no corresponding instances of the child entity. And that brings up an interesting situation.

For illustration's sake, let's define a couple of entities in a P -|---o- P association:

Entity	Relationship	Instances	Attributes
COMIC CHARACTER	parent	Tom, Jerry	*Does it really matter?*
NATURE	child	cat, dog	hair, tail

In other words,

1. Each COMIC CHARACTER has zero or one NATURE.
2. Tom and Jerry are instances of COMIC CHARACTER.
3. Cat and dog are instances of NATURE.

Now, let's say that

- Tom is associated with *cat.*
- Jerry has no association. (After all, association is optional.)

If we combine COMIC and NATURE so that all the attributes of NATURE become attributes of COMIC, then Tom has values for the attributes that had been associated with the instance *cat*: *hair*=gray, *tail*=yes. But Jerry has nulls for the attributes *hair* and *tail*.

That is to say, the attributes *hair* and *tail* are optional, and we've already noted that, with respect to attributes, optionality ("Add later") is at least a yellow flag. So a P-to-optional-P association may be a signal to look for secondary entities or, more generally, to look further into the business reality. If the association is truly optional-becoming-mandatory, the presence of nulls is probably no problem. But if not, you may be combining entities only to have to break them up again during normalization.

And then there are times when you may want to maintain two entities as a look-ahead to physical data modeling. Consider a distributed database: different tables (bodies of information) on different servers. You might want to store the basic data—say, binary objects like picture files—in a table residing on a server that has been optimized for large files like that. Then you could set up an index on another server.

For example, a Human Resources database might put employee pictures on a special server. The table there would handle just two datatypes: the one used by the picture files (binary large object - BLOB) and the one for the primary key (character, autonumber, or the like). The main server would have all the tables needed to handle HR information, including at least one table relating employee_id# to selection attributes (indexes) and the foreign key copied down to the picture table. That foreign key gives access to the employee's picture.

6.   NEW NOTIONS

entity cycle, triad, multiple associations, parallel intersecting entities

Chapter 10

VALIDATING THE DATA MODEL

Wherein we prove our worth

You've arrived! This is where we discuss normalization.

We can look at normalization from at least three related points of view:

- As a set of rules that inform your data modeling decisions throughout your work.
- As a validation process: matching the product against standards. When it comes to data modeling, the basic standards are called the **normal forms**.
- As a process of progressive correction: bringing the product into conformity with each normal form in turn.

If you've done your modeling correctly and completely, with a good up-front understanding and awareness of normalization rules, your model should be valid at least to Third normal form (3NF). Thus, normalization should be validation: a matter of checking each entity against the criteria for each normal form.

As correction, normalization is a painful process, but it may be necessary if you're wrestling with an existing database—i.e., doing reverse engineering. You examine a table, its columns, and its rows, testing your findings against the standard (the normal form). As you find discrepancies, you may define new columns or move existing columns to other tables, creating them as necessary. Normalizing one table may entail creating or changing other tables, which must be tested or even retested. When the database passes the tests of one normal form, you start again, testing against the next higher normal form.

Obviously, validation is easier than correction. If you build your model carefully and thoroughly, you'll be creating attributes, entities, and entity structures that are already normalized, and this is a significant advantage to building logical data models our way, with patterns (discussed in the next chapter). When you validate them (the attributes, entities, and entity structures), they'll pass without change, and everybody's happy.

1. DEPENDENCIES

Normalization applies to the attributes of an entity, not to its associations. When we talk about the **dependency** of one attribute on another,[52] we mean that the value of one attribute is determined by the value of another: if you know the one value, you know the other.

The most obvious example is the dependency of attributes on the entity's primary key. Given 5 as the value of <u>artist id#</u>, you can know immediately that the artist's name is Albrecht Altdorfer, that he was born circa 1480, and that he died in 1538. Another value for <u>artist id#</u> gives particular values for artist_name, artist_birth_date, and artist_death_date—values that may or may not be the same as for Mr. Altdorfer, values that may even be null, but values no less determinate for that. (Another way we talk about dependencies is to say that one attribute **determines** the value of one or more others: it is the **determinant** of the other attributes' values.)

What applies to a simple primary key applies also to a compound primary key. Take the role entity ORGANIZATION ROLE. We know that it has the compound primary key <u>org no#</u>, <u>org type no#</u>. Given values for those two components of the key, we can find a particular value of the attribute organization_role_start_date—say, "20010301" (March 1, 2001).

Note that we can't get that start date by knowing the value of <u>org no#</u> or <u>org type no#</u> alone. The attribute organization_role_start_date is dependent on the whole key.

---

[52] The following discussion is indebted to Rob and Semaan 2004: Chapter 2; and to Reingruber and Gregory 1994: Chapter 8.

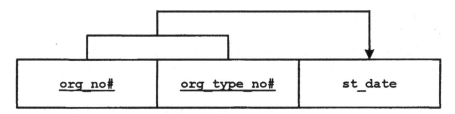

org no#	org type no#	st_date

If, however, an attribute depends on only one of those component keys, we say that it is **partially functionally dependent**. Imagine that we've given the attribute organization_type_name to ORGANIZATION ROLE. If we have a value for the entire compound primary key, we can find out the value for organization_type_name. All well and good.

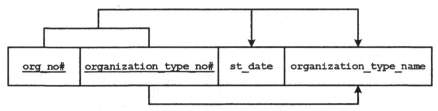

org no#	organization type no#	st_date	organization_type_name

But look again: we can find that value if we have only the value of organization type no#. That's what we mean by **partial functional dependency**: only part of the primary key determines the value of the other attribute. (Yes, you're right: organization_type_name should be in the type entity, not the role entity. That's the kind of error you catch when you identify dependencies like this.)

Finally, there are cases where one or more attributes depend on another attribute and the determinant is *not* all or even part of the entity's primary key. We call that a **transitive dependency**.

Let's imagine that ORGANIZATION ROLE has another couple of attributes: product_code and product_name:

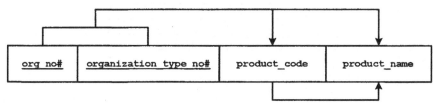

org no#	organization type no#	product_code	product_name

If we know product-code, we know product_name, and thus we have a transitive dependency. Note that product_code could be a foreign key—but not part of the primary key—and we'd still have a transitive dependency.

2. REDUNDANCY

Data redundancy, as used here, has nothing to do with backups and data security. Those kinds of redundancy are valuable. Data redundancy is a problem.

Data redundancy exists when we have a particular value of an attribute turning up many times. Each time an instance of the entity is created, someone—often a human being—had to enter a value for that attribute. And people make mistakes, noise creeps in, and things become messy.[53]

On the other hand, if that human being enters a value only once, well, we're happy: the value may be right, or it may be wrong, but at least it's stable. And if it's wrong, it only has to be corrected once, not hundreds or even thousands of times.

It's pretty obvious that data redundancy is going to happen if we have partial functional dependencies. To repeat, partial functional dependency happens when an attribute is not dependent on all the parts of a compound primary key. Let's look at a familiar example, ORGANIZATION ROLE:

org_no#	org_type_no#	org_type_name
1	1	vendor
2	2	customer
3	3	contractor
4	1	vendor
5	2	customer
1	3	contractor
2	1	vendor
3	2	customer
4	3	contractor
5	1	vendor
1	2	customer
2	3	contractor
3	1	vendor
4	2	customer
5	3	contractor

---

[53] When we talk about different instances of an entity having "the same" value or a "particular" value for an attribute, we're speaking in semantic terms. To a computer, "Gauguin" and "Guaguin" are different strings, and that's all it knows. But in semantic terms, one's the correct spelling of the artist's name, the other is a misspelling, and we have redundant data.

<u>org no#</u>, <u>org type no#</u> is our compound primary key, and org_type_no# determines org_type_name, so we have a partial functional dependency.

The maximum number of instances of ORGANIZATION ROLE is the number of values of <u>org no#</u> (5) multiplied by the number of values of <u>org type no#</u> (3).[54] If we have three values of <u>org type no#</u>, we have three values of org_type_name: that's our partial functional dependency at work. We have five copies of that attribute pair repeated in the instances of ORGANIZATION ROLE. And that, folks, is data redundancy.

In the case of transitive dependencies, the argument is more intuitive, but the result is the same. We're going to recognize a transitive dependency only if it happens a number of times, and if it happens a number of times, what we've got is redundant data.

Let's look at a case of transitive dependency. We've got an old Artworks database table that includes pretty much everything that can be said about a work of art. Every time Giuseppe Arcimboldo's name appears in the Artist_ID column, "1527?-1593" appears in the Birth_Death column, and we have half a dozen or more of his paintings listed in the table. That's a good chunk of redundant data.

Work_ID	Title	Artist_ID	Birth_Death	Creation_Date
15	Spring	Giuseppe Arcimboldo	1527?-1593	
16	Spring	Giuseppe Arcimboldo	1527?-1593	
17	Summer	Giuseppe Arcimboldo	1527?-1593	1573
18	Autumn	Giuseppe Arcimboldo	1527?-1593	1573
19	Winter	Giuseppe Arcimboldo	1527?-1593	1573
20	Fire	Giuseppe Arcimboldo	1527?-1593	1566
21	Water	Giuseppe Arcimboldo	1527?-1593	1566
22	Winter	Giuseppe Arcimboldo	1527?-1593	
23	Summer	Giuseppe Arcimboldo	1527?-1593	1563

Note the problems:

- Each time one of Mr. Arcimboldo's paintings is **added** to the list, someone has to spell "Arcimboldo." Or is it "Archimboldo"? "Arcimboldi"? Actually, all three spellings appear in the art history literature.
- If we don't standardize on one spelling—"Arcimboldo," for instance—what happens when users start searching? For one thing,

---

[54] With a compound primary key, each component has to have more than one possible value.

they have to be good spellers: there's no nice drop-down selection menu. Second, if they search for "Arcimboldo," they miss retrieving the paintings by Mr. Archimboldo and Mr. Arcimboldi.

- One Mr. Arcimboldo has "1527?-1593" for his birth and death dates. Another might have "1527-1593," and another (a true artistic prodigy) might have "1527?-1539." It's that old gremlin, human error, introducing even more variation into our table.
- As we start **updating** the table, correcting the errors and standardizing our data, we end up doing a lot of data entry. There are a lot of values to be changed, and with every change comes, again, the possibility of error. And when the job's done, someone comes along and adds another record: the more records, the more errors, and the more consequences down the line.
- If this were a matter of partial functional dependency, with Artist_ID as part of the primary key, we'd have still more problems. After all, the primary key is marked, "Add now, cannot modify later." We couldn't change "Archimboldo" to "Arcimboldo" at all: we'd have to **delete** the entire row—all that beautiful data—and then enter everything again.

What we're talking about is **data anomalies**:

- Errors that propagate as records are added are called **insertion anomalies**.
- Errors that propagate as records are updated are called **update anomalies**.
- Errors that propagate as records are deleted are called **deletion anomalies**.

But not all data redundancy comes from partial or transitive dependencies. Take a look at the Artworks database table from another view:

Work_ID	Title	Creation_Date	Artist_ID	Museum_ID
1	Holy Trinity	1555	Alessandro Allori	SS Annunziata
2	Venus and Adonis		Alessandro Allori	Pitti Palace
3	Hercules and the Muses		Alessandro Allori	Uffizi
4	Venus and Cupid		Alessandro Allori	Uffizi
5	Bianca Cappello		Alessandro Allori	Uffizi

Work_ID	Title	Creation_Date	Artist_ID	Museum_ID
6	Birth of Mary	ca. 1520	Albrecht Altdorfer	Alte Pinakothek
7	Susanna in the Bath	1526	Albrecht Altdorfer	Alte Pinakothek
8	Battle of Issus	1529	Albrecht Altdorfer	Alte Pinakothek
9	Danube Landscape with Castle Wörth	after 1520	Albrecht Altdorfer	Alte Pinakothek
10	Judith with the Head of Holofernes		Cristofano Allori	Pitti Palace
11	Baby Jesus asleep on the Cross		Cristofano Allori	Pitti Palace
12	Annunciation	ca. 1430	Fra Angelico	Prado
13	Coronation of the Virgin		Fra Angelico	Uffizi
14	St Anthony Abbot		Fra Angelico	Museum of Fine Arts, Houston
15	Spring		Giuseppe Arcimboldo	Academia de Bellas Artes de San Fernando
16	Spring		Giuseppe Arcimboldo	Louvre
17	Summer	1573	Giuseppe Arcimboldo	Louvre
18	Autumn	1573	Giuseppe Arcimboldo	Louvre
19	Winter	1573	Giuseppe Arcimboldo	Louvre
20	Fire	1566	Giuseppe Arcimboldo	Kunsthistorisches
21	Water	1566	Giuseppe Arcimboldo	Kunsthistorisches

Notice that, while each record is different, there are quite a few repeated values:

- In the *Title* column, one value is repeated twice out of 21 instances.
- In the *Creation_Date* column, two values are repeated. (total: 5)
- In the *Artist_ID* column, five values are repeated. (total: 21)
- In the *Museum_ID* column, five values are repeated. (total: 17)

If we were looking at this table as an assemblage of character data, we might be tempted to decide that we have some transitive dependencies: Albrecht Altdorfer's paintings are in the Alte Pinakothek, while Cristofano Allori's are in the Pitti Palace.

But behind the table is the entity: behind the physical database is the logical data model, and behind the model is business reality. If we ask a subject matter expert about these "transitive dependencies," they dissolve: What happens if we add a record for another of Mr. Altdorfer's paintings, and (as is quite possible) it's in the Kunsthistorisches Museum in Vienna? Nonetheless, we have data redundancy, and we need at least to reduce it to a manageable minimum.

What isn't redundant data? Well, foreign keys exist in more than one entity. In fact, during normalization (if not before), you are adding more entities, increasing the number of copies of foreign keys across the database. Difference is, the values of a foreign key are not normally entered individually, from outside the database: the database application copies them exactly from their origin, the originating primary key in the parent table. So foreign keys are not redundant data in themselves, though a foreign key may be the determinant in a partial functional or transitive dependency.

3.   THE NORMAL FORMS

The database people have a venerable adage:

"The key, the whole key, and nothing but the key, so help me Codd."[55]

The phrase is a reminder of the first three normal forms:

- "The key" = First normal form
- "The whole key" = Second normal form
- "Nothing but the key" = Third normal form.

Another of their crude mnemonic tricks is the acronym *RPT*:

R   First normal form: No **R**epeating Groups
P   Second normal form: No **P**artial Functional Dependencies
T   Third normal form: No **T**ransitive Dependencies.

As you read about the normal forms, you'll see how these phrases apply.

[55] Edgar F. Codd first proposed the use of mathematical relations for managing data.

3.1 First normal form (1NF)

"The key"/"No repeating groups"

To satisfy the standard for First normal form, every entity in the data model has to satisfy three criteria:

1. **Integrity.** The primary key has to be unique in the model: no other entity (except secondary entities) may use the same attribute or set of attributes as its primary key.
2. **Dependency.** All generic non-key attributes in the entity must depend on the primary key. By "generic" we mean that the key is not a selection attribute, a group attribute, or a repeating group attribute.
3. **Single value.** For every instance in the entity, the instance may have one and only one value for each attribute.

Let's take a quick look at these criteria.

1. The integrity rule for primary keys is just a special case of the general attribute uniqueness rule: a non-key attribute may exist in only one entity in the logical data model.
2. A secondary entity's primary key is at the same time a foreign key, and foreign keys are excluded from the attribute uniqueness rule. In "business terms," a secondary entity is an extension of its parent (supertype) entity. It provides information about a category (subset) of instances in the parent entity. The parent entity does the real accounting, while the secondary entity adds values for attributes that are relevant only to that category of the parent.
3. The dependency rule essentially says that the primary key must be the primary key: If we have a value for the primary key, we can find the corresponding value for any other attribute in the entity. Note that the dependency rule for First normal form does not rule out other, coexisting dependencies: dependency on an alternate (candidate) key, partial functional dependencies, or transitive dependencies. Just wait, though ...
4. The single value rule comes from the limitations of relational databases, which work with two-dimensional tables. If you think in terms of a table, the single value rule says that each cell can contain only one value.

Thus, there's one thing you need to do to bring an entity into conformity with the 1NF standard. You will have to take any repeating group attributes and create a new entity for each of them.

Let's go back to an old example. Here's ARTWORK as a table:

artwork_id#	artwork_name	artwork_subject
1	Terranuova Madonna	Mary, Christ Child, saint, landscape
2	Baptism of Christ	Christ, saint, angel, landscape
3	Allegory of Time and Love	Venus, Cupid

As long as artwork-subject exists in its current form, ARTWORK is not in First normal form. So what if we move artwork_subject into a new entity called SUBJECT? As a table, our entity looks like this:

artwork_subject_no#	artwork_subject
1	Mary
2	Christ Child
3	saint
4	landscape
5	Christ
6	angel
7	Venus
8	Cupid

Now we can check our entities against our Business Statements:

"Each ARTWORK may have zero, one, or many SUBJECTs.
"Each SUBJECT must apply to one or many ARTWORKs."

In other words, ARTWORK >|---o< SUBJECT.

Well, we know what to do about this situation:

ARTWORK -|---o< ARTWORK SUBJECT >|---|- SUBJECT

We create an intersecting entity, ARTWORK SUBJECT, that's going to look like this, tablewise:

artwork_id#	artwork_subject_no#
1	1
1	2
1	3
1	4
2	5
2	3
2	6
2	4
3	7
3	8

And so it goes: every time you come across a repeating group attribute, you're going to have to break it out into another entity. And anytime you make a change like this, you'll need to go back and find a Business Statement that validates it. If one doesn't exist, talk to the subject matter experts. They may confirm your decisions, or they may have information pointing you toward a different solution.

3.2 Second normal form (2NF)

"The whole key"/"No partial functional dependencies"

The rules for Second normal form are few and sweet:

1. The entity must meet the standard of First normal form.
2. The entity must have no partial functional dependencies. In other words, all dependencies on a compound primary key must be dependencies on the whole key, not on any fraction of the key.

With a partial functional dependency, there are two possible cases, and there's a pretty direct way of dealing with each.

Case 1: The determinant attribute in the partial functional dependency is a foreign key. The usual solution is to move the dependent attribute out of the current entity and into the parent entity of the foreign key.

We've seen this before, with ORGANIZATION ROLE:

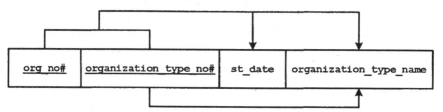

The <u>organization type no#</u> component has been copied down from the ORGANIZATION TYPE entity. Since organization_type_name is dependent on <u>organization type no#</u>, it seems only reasonable to move organization_type_name into the ORGANIZATION TYPE entity as well.

Of course, in another situation the foreign key might have been copied down from a secondary entity. Thus, it may be two or three levels away from the originating (principal) entity. Moving the dependent attribute up to the immediate parent entity may make business sense, or it may not: our fallen sparrow may have to fly up the inheritance tree branch by branch before it finds a nest.

Case 2: The determinant attribute is not a foreign key. For example, MEDIA has a two-part primary key, and neither part exists elsewhere in the data model:

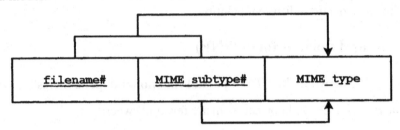

We have a partial functional dependency here: if we know the MIME subtype (jpg, gif, etc.), we know the MIME type. And we know that getting rid of the partial functional dependency means moving MIME_type elsewhere. But where?

Simple solution: Create a new static principal entity called MIME. The attribute MIME-subtype becomes MIME's primary key, and MIME_type becomes a non-key attribute:

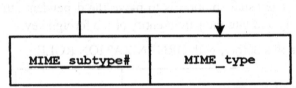

The next step: Connect MEDIA to MIME. The subject matter expert says that

1. A media item may come in a variety of flavors—for example, AG002.jpg, AG002.gif, even AG002.wav—but it must come in at least one flavor.
2. Many media files have the same extension—AG002.jpg, AG003.jpg, etc.—but each extension must be represented by at least one image file.

This tells us that there's a mandatory-many-to-mandatory-many association between MEDIA and MIME: MEDIA >|---|< MIME. But when we set up MIME as a table, we'll want to populate it at the outset with a number of standard type/subtype pairs, so that they'll be there when we start adding media file records to MEDIA. With a >|---|< association, data entry is not possible: we are locked out. So we'll modify the association: make it MEDIA >o---|< MIME. The association must be made optional (or optional becoming mandatory) on at least one side to allow us to populate the tables.

Final step: Create an intersecting entity, MEDIA MIME. Thus we have

MEDIA -|---|< MEDIA MIME >o---|- MIME

MEDIA MIME has a compound primary key: <u>filename#</u>, <u>MIME subtype#</u>. So if we want to find all the file flavors for a particular filename, we just look in MEDIA MIME and find the corresponding instances.

So, in sum, to resolve a partial functional dependency in Case 2, you

- Create a new entity.
- Move the partial functional dependency—determinant and dependent attributes—into the new entity.
- Define the association between old entity and new, based on business rules.
- Create meta-entities as necessary.

There's one last step: you need to test each changed entity against the standard (1NF *and* 2NF). It's not uncommon for a change to create new problems or expose hidden business rules.

3.3 Third normal form (3NF)

"Nothing but the key"/"No transitive dependencies"

Here's the Third normal form standard:

1. The entity meets the Second normal form standard (which means it automatically meets the First normal form standard as well).
2. The entity contains no transitive dependencies.

The usual solution for transitive dependencies is pretty much the same as for partial functional dependencies, Case 2 in Section 3.2 (above): The transitive dependency is spun off into a new entity, the primary key and remaining attributes stay with the original entity, and all associations have to be reassessed.

Here's a simple example. The old, everything-but-the-kitchen-sink artworks database has attributes like these:

- <u>work no#</u>
- title
- creation_date
- artist_name
- artist_pseudonym.

If we know artist_name, we know artist_pseudonym: Michelangelo Merisi is always Caravaggio, and vice versa. So (assuming artist_name is not a key) we have a transitive dependency.

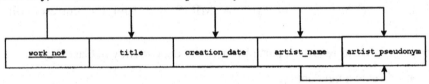

We resolve the dependency by creating a new entity, ARTIST. It will have the attributes

- <u>artist id#</u> (Let's do this right: by creating a unique primary key, we allow artist_name to be recycled with many different artist_pseudonyms.)
- artist_name
- artist-pseudonym.

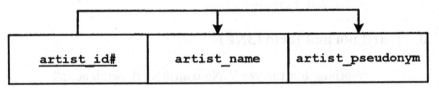

And, having created this new entity, we give it a little thought. While an artist may have only one given name, he or she may have a number of pseudonyms. So we need to break out another entity: ARTIST PSEUDONYM. The association between ARTIST is one-to-many. (It seems unlikely that two artists will have the same pseudonym. In that case, we'd have a many-to-many association.)

So, from our old artworks database we come up with three tables. ARTIST will look like this:

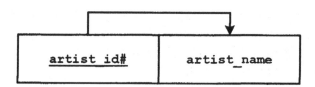

ARTIST PSEUDONYM is the big winner. It gets a primary key, <u>artist pseudonym id#</u>, and as a child entity it inherits a foreign key from ARTIST:

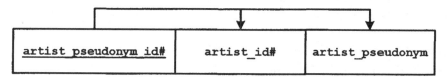

That leaves the following attributes in the ARTWORK entity:

- <u>work no#</u>
- title
- creation_date.

Since each ARTIST makes one or many ARTWORKs, ARTWORK is also a child entity and likewise inherits a foreign key from ARTIST:

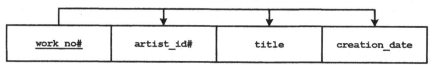

The problem with the original transitive dependency was that every time we added another painting by Caravaggio to our ARTWORK table, we'd have to type out "Michelangelo Merisi" and "Caravaggio." Lots of chances for error. Now that we've created ARTIST and ARTIST PSEUDONYM, we type these names only once. Problem solved. (Hold on! you say. What if an artwork is created by more than one artist? Well, change the problem, change the solution.)

A final note

If, after everything else, you still have derived attributes, your entity isn't in 3NF. After all, a derived attribute is dependent on at least one other attribute.

- If the determinant attribute is part of the primary key, you've got a partial functional dependency.
- If the determinant is a non-key attribute in the same entity, you've got a transitive dependency.

- And if the determinant is elsewhere, your derived attribute may be in the wrong entity.
- Things get even more complicated if the derived attribute depends on more than one other attribute.

Luckily, like foreign keys, derived attributes don't create data redundancy problems. They are calculated by formula or by aggregation. They are not input, they aren't used as primary keys, and thus they do not create insertion, update, or deletion anomalies. So, if derived attributes are the only reason your entities aren't in 3NF, this is nothing to worry about.

3.4 Boyce/Codd normal form, Fourth normal form, Fifth normal form, and beyond

Usually, if you can get your model to 3NF, you're in good shape. Beyond 3NF, you encounter the higher normal forms. But you don't usually run into situations where you need them, and we won't do more than just describe them here.

Boyce/Codd normal form (BCNF) addresses some special cases of partial functional or transitive dependencies. That's why it is often combined with 2NF or 3NF, and entities that are in 3NF are almost always in BCNF as well.

In brief, BCNF looks at cases where

1. There are two or more candidate keys.
2. The candidate keys are compound keys.
3. The candidate keys share at least one key attribute in common.

For example, AB#→C,D and AC#→B,D, where A, B, C, and D are all the attributes in our entity (and → means "determines").

Fourth normal form (4NF) addresses cases of **multivalued dependency** (MVD). These are situations in which A#→B and A#→C, where B and C are repeating group attributes. Sometimes B→C, and that's where the problems arise. Generally, though, if an entity is 1NF, it is also 4NF.

Fifth normal form (5NF) addresses cases of **join dependency** (a situation that may happen during earlier normalization processes):

- Starting with a single entity, we set out to resolve repeating group attributes, partial functional dependencies, and/or transitive dependencies, and we produce three or more new entities.

- If we then associate those entities with a new entity and, by proper inheritance of keys, recreate the data of our original entity, no new information—no new instances—may be created in the process.

In other words, the original is equal to the sum (join) of its parts. That's 5NF.

Other normal forms have been defined as well, including Domain Key normal form, in which no anomalies exist.

4. NEW NOTIONS

dependency, determinant, partial functional dependency, transitive dependency, data redundancy, data anomaly, insertion anomaly, update anomaly, deletion anomaly, First normal form, Second normal form, Third normal form, Boyce/Codd normal form, Fourth normal form, Fifth normal form, Domain Key normal form, multivalued dependency, join dependency.

Chapter 11

DESIGN PATTERNS

Common shapes for common situations

The notion of **design patterns** has become commonplace in object oriented software development, and a few data modelers have applied it to their area of expertise. A design pattern is defined variously as

- "a set of rules describing how to accomplish certain tasks" (Pree and Gamma 1995: 61)
- "a reusable implementation model or architecture that can be applied to solve a particular recurring class of problem" (Alpert and Brown 1998: 2)
- a "structured, packaged problem solution in literary form," "a form for documenting best practices," "a rule of thumb," "a template"—in short, a way of "capturing and expressing the developer's tacit knowledge" (Evitts 2000: 2, 16)
- a "description … of communicating objects and classes that are customized to solve a general design problem in a particular context." (Gamma *et al.* 1995: 27)

The notion of design patterns derives from architecture. According to Christopher Alexander, "Each pattern describes a problem which occurs over and over again in our environment, and then describes the core of the solution to that problem, in such a way that you can use this solution a million times over, without ever doing it the same way twice" (Alexander *et al.* 1977: x).

Design patterns give names to practical knowledge; they define a high-level vocabulary for understanding and solving business statements graphically. Design patterns are presented in a standard format; they're like recipes in a cookbook or dress patterns in a catalog. Above all, they are practical, first as instructional materials and then as development tools.

Below, we've defined eight data modeling design patterns. Each pattern is presented in the following format:

- Name – Actually, an acronym
- Intent – The purpose of the pattern
- Structure – A diagram and explanation
- Discussion – Where the pattern applies, how it works, its advantages, and any adaptations; with one or more analyzed examples
- Collaboration – How the pattern combines with other patterns
- Implementation – Variations, their advantages and disadvantages, with examples
- Sample – An application presented and discussed
- Closely Related Patterns – Itemized.

Sometimes, topics will be combined or omitted. Note, too, that for clarification's sake we often talk about entities as if they were tables, even though we're talking logical data modeling, not physical database design.

If you've mastered everything said in this book to this point, the data modeling design patterns should be a good review and summary. In the field, they should provide a shorthand for doing data modeling on the fly, in meetings with executive management or subject matter experts. If you know the patterns and the key structure for each pattern, you can save time, save pain, and avoid mistakes.

1.   NAME: P   PATTERN 1

1.1 Intent

Represent a single principal entity; map one noun.

1.2 Structure

```
┌─────────────────────┐
│                     │
│      ARTWORK        │
│                     │
└─────────────────────┘
```

1.3 Discussion, Collaboration, Implementation

P ("principal") is the simplest pattern and the first entity flavor laid down for any larger pattern. It will have an originating unique primary key, expressed in one or more columns. It will also have at least one non-key attribute column. Otherwise, it's useless: a mere list of identifiers that don't identify anything.

P comes in two versions:

- Dynamic P: instances are added, changed, or deleted frequently
- Static P: instances are seldom added, changed, or deleted.

P may constitute an entire database, with no associations or related entities.

1.4 Sample

As an entire physical database unto itself, a single-table database, ARTWORK might look like this:

artwork_id#	title	artist	location	comment
1	The Crowning with Thorns	Anthony van Dyck	Madrid, Prado	Composition based on a prototype by Titian.
2	The Redeemer	Titian	Florence, Pitti Palace	Painted for the Duke of Urbino.

1.5 Closely Related Patterns

All other patterns: none of the other patterns can exist without a P entity.

2.   NAME: PP   PATTERN 2

2.1   Intent

Associate two or more dynamic principal entities in one or more one-to-many relationships; map two or more nouns

2.2   Structure

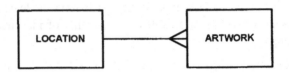

2.3   Discussion, Collaboration

PP ("principal to principal") is the association of two or more P patterns. Therefore, each entity follows the P rules: one originating unique primary key of one or more columns, at least one non-key attribute column.

Note that one or more Ps are parent to one or more other Ps. Therefore, the child Ps will have one or more foreign key columns. These columns will receive the primary keys of the parent entity or entities. The parent P may be either static or dynamic. The child P is almost always dynamic.

PP may constitute the entire physical database, or it may be part of a larger pattern.

2.4   Implementation

This is a simple PP pattern (or, if you prefer, a pair of PP patterns). Each AGENT has one or many CLIENTs, and each CLIENT has one or many ACCOUNTs. The agent's primary key value is copied down into a foreign key column, into the appropriate cell in each instance representing a client served by that agent. Likewise, the client's primary key value will copy down as a foreign key into the appropriate cell in every row of ACCOUNT that represents an account owned by that client. If the AGENT-CLIENT association is identifying, AGENT's primary key will be copied down to ACCOUNT.

Here's another implementation:

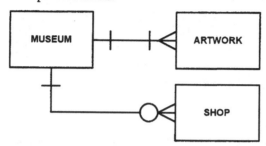

Here, the two PP patterns model two different relationships with MUSEUM:

- Each MUSEUM holds one or many ARTWORKs.
- Each MUSEUM may have zero, one, or many SHOPs.

If the association between MUSEUM and ARTWORK is identifying, MUSEUM's primary key will copy down as part of ARTWORK's compound primary key. That is as much as to say: "This work of art is identified with this museum."

In the second association, SHOP may receive MUSEUM's primary key as a foreign key pure and simple (not as part of SHOP's primary key) in a non-identifying association. Consider that a shop may be part of a chain of shops. Therefore, though a particular shop will be in one and only one museum, shops in the chain may be in many. To look at the situation another way, there may be a CHAIN entity that has a mandatory-one-to-optional-many association with SHOP: a particular shop may or may not be part of a chain. SHOP might in this case have a primary key column and two foreign key columns, one receiving MUSEUM's primary key, the other CHAIN's primary key.

2.5 Sample

Let's consider the PP pattern LOCATION -|---< ARTWORK. LOCATION will probably have attributes like

location_id#	location_name	location_city	location_country
1	Prado	Madrid	Spain
2	Pitti Palace	Florence	Italy

ARTWORK will have attributes like these:

artwork_id#	location_id#	title	artist	comment
1	1	The Crowning with Thorns	Anthony van Dyck	Composition based on a prototype by Titian.
2	2	The Redeemer	Titian	Painted for the Duke of Urbino.

The pattern's optionalities can be

- Mandatory: Every LOCATION is associated with one or many ARTWORKs. *OR*
- Optional: Every LOCATION is associated with zero, one, or many ARTWORKs. *OR*
- Optional-becoming-mandatory: Every LOCATION may currently be associated with zero, one, or many ARTWORKs, but it will eventually be associated with one or many ARTWORKs.

Optional or optional-becoming-mandatory is probably the most convenient way to define the association for database purposes. It lets you enter a number of locations at one sitting, then associate the artworks to them at your leisure.

2.6   Closely Related Patterns

P

3.   NAME: PIP   PATTERN 3

3.1   Intent

Resolve a many-to-many association between two or more dynamic principal entities.

3.2 Structure

3.3 Discussion

With PIP ("principal-intersecting-principal"), the two or more dynamic principal entities conform to the P pattern: each has one originating unique primary key of one or more columns, and each has at least one non-key attribute column. The PI associations may be mandatory, optional, or optional-becoming-mandatory.

The PI associations are identifying. The intersecting entity receives a copy of the complete primary key from each principal entity. These two or more foreign keys are all (or part) of the intersecting entity's unique compound primary key.

The intersecting entity may also have one or more non-key attributes.

3.4 Collaboration, Implementation

PIP may constitute the entire physical database, or it may be part of a larger pattern. For example, one or all Ps might be mixed secondary/principal entities. In other words, P might be a secondary entity—a subset—of a principal entity while having secondary entities of its own, to break down its own contents into subsets. The intersecting entity would relate all the instances of P, and only those, to the instances of every other P (which might in turn be a subset of yet another principal entity).

3.5 Sample

Let's consider this PIP:

The reality is "An artist may create one or many artworks, and an artwork may be created by one or many artists."

The optionality of the associations may be

- Mandatory: Every ARTIST must relate to one or many ARTWORKs, and vice versa. *OR*
- Optional: Every ARTIST may relate to zero, one, or many ARTWORKs, and vice versa. *OR*
- Optional-becoming-mandatory: Every ARTIST will eventually relate to one or many ARTWORKs, and vice versa.

As with PP, designating the optionality as optional or optional-becoming-mandatory gives us more flexibility in populating the tables.

Typical attributes for the entities will look like this:

- ARTIST: artist_id#, artist_name, etc.
- ARTWORK: artwork_id#, artwork_name, artwork_date, etc.
- ARTWORK ARTIST: artwork_id#, artist_id#.

The primary keys are copied down from the principal entities and become components of the intersecting entity's compound primary key.

Let's say, for example, that the ARTIST table looks like this—

artist_id#	artist_name
1	Anthony van Dyck
2	Frans Snyders

—and let's say that the ARTWORK table looks like this:

artwork_id#	artwork_name
1	Fish Market
2	Rest on the Flight to Egypt

ARTWORK ARTIST would look like this:

artwork_id#	artist_id#
1	1
2	1
1	2

That is to say, van Dyck painted *Rest on the Flight to Egypt,* and he and Snyders collaborated on *Fish Market.*

Note that each pair of IDs (foreign keys) in ARTWORK ARTIST is unique. It's got to be this way: the two foreign keys together constitute the primary key, which must be unique. In situations where the two-part primary key is not unique, an additional key column or columns may be added.

We could add one or more non-key attributes to ARTWORK ARTIST, perhaps to characterize the relationship between the artist and the artwork.

3.6 Closely Related Patterns

None

---

4. NAME: PU   PATTERN 4

4.1 Intent

Associate two instances of the same dynamic principal entity; model two instances of the same noun in a one-to-one, one-to-many, or many-to-many association.

4.2 Structure

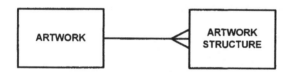

4.3 Discussion

The structure entity resolves recursive relationships, where instances of the dynamic principal entity have associations with each other. The P table has the characteristics already defined: one originating unique primary key of one or more columns and at least one non-key attribute column. Note that P's primary key may itself be compound.

Each instance of U associates exactly two instances of P. Thus, the U table will have two or more columns of foreign keys. It may also have a non-key attribute column for naming or describing how the two instances of P relate to each other.

4.4 Collaboration, Implementation

PU may constitute the entire physical database, or it may be part of a larger pattern. A PU database would have two tables, of course. P might look like this:

artwork_id#	artwork_name
1	Nicolaes van der Meer
2	Cornelia Vooght Claesdr.
3	Willem Coymans
4	Martin Luther
5	Katherine Bora

And U might look like this, with artwork_id# (1) and artwork_id# (2) constituting the compound primary key:

artwork_id# (1)	artwork_id# (2)	artwork_relationship
1	2	pendant
4	5	pendant

In this small database, we have five instances of artworks. Four of them are related to others as pendants (paintings created to be displayed as a pair). Note that the "pendant" association is one-to-one-optional: an artwork may have zero or one association, but no more than one.

But let's add some more instances:

artwork_id#	artwork_name
1	Nicolaes van der Meer
2	Cornelia Vooght Claesdr.
3	Willem Coymans
4	Martin Luther
5	Katherine Bora
6	The Gloomy Day
7	Hay Harvest
8	Corn Harvest
9	Return of the herd
10	Hunters in the Snow

artwork_id# (1)	artwork_id# (2)	artwork_relationship
1	2	pendant
4	5	pendant
6	7	The Seasons
6	8	The Seasons
6	9	The Seasons
6	10	The Seasons
7	8	The Seasons

artwork_id# (1)	artwork_id# (2)	artwork_relationship
7	9	The Seasons
7	10	The Seasons
8	9	The Seasons
8	10	The Seasons
9	10	The Seasons

The association between P and U in this case is one-to-optional-many: each instance of P may have zero, one, or many associations with other instances of P. The list of instances in U tells us that the portrait of Nicolaes van der Meer is the pendant to the portrait of Cornelia Vooght Claesdr. The portrait of Willem Coymans has no relationship with any other painting; thus, its artwork_id# does not appear in either of the foreign key columns in U.

As for the five Bruegel paintings in P (artwork_id# 6, 7, 8, 9, and 10), all are part of a series depicting the seasons. To ensure that all five paintings are properly associated, we need ten rows in the U table. You can test this by verifying that every possible combination of two Bruegel paintings appears only once in U: 6 and 7 (*The Gloomy Day* and *Hay Harvest*) appears once and only once, etc.

Now let's look at an example of the PU pattern as part of a larger structure:

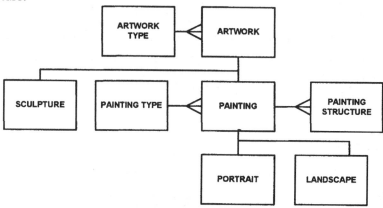

The entities PAINTING and PAINTING STRUCTURE constitute the PU pattern. PAINTING is both a secondary and a principal entity: it is a secondary entity with respect to ARTWORK, and it has secondary entities of its own. PAINTING TYPE identifies those secondary entities. PAINTING STRUCTURE associates instances of PAINTING.

Note that

1. It doesn't matter whether two associated instances are both portraits or both landscapes, or one landscape and one portrait.
2. If all associations are between portraits, we are *not* going to change our map. PORTRAIT does not need a U of its own. After all, portraits are paintings, and PAINTING STRUCTURE can handle the associations quite well.
3. If we want to associate a painting with a sculpture, we have to create a new PU pattern by creating ARTWORK STRUCTURE and associating it with ARTWORK.

As keys go,

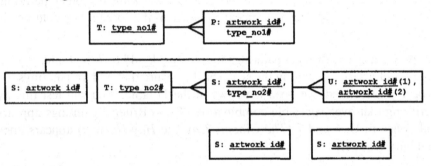

ARTWORK's primary key, artwork id#, copies down as an originating primary key to its children and its grandchildren. The primary keys of the two type entities copy down to their associated principal entities as foreign keys. As for PAINTING, the entity that is P and S at the same time, its primary key copies down to U twice, once for each of the two instances that are being associated. Thus, U has a compound primary key in two parts. Note that the primary key in PAINTING is not originating, but is copied down from ARTWORK.

4.5 Sample

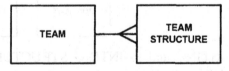

Here's a model of a schedule for baseball games. Each team is represented as an instance in the principal entity, TEAM:

team_id#	team_name
1	New York Yankees
2	Houston Astros
3	Laramie Elks

We can define a baseball game as a contest between two teams. The U entity (we've called it TEAM STRUCTURE, but we could as easily call it GAME) can then be used as a schedule of games:

team_id# (1)	team_id# (2)	game_date
1	2	2004-06-01
2	3	2004-06-07
1	3	2004-06-10

Of course, this simple model has its limits. It's going to be a very short summer if no team can play any other team more than once.

4.6   Closely Related Patterns

TPSSU

---

5.   NAME: TPSS   PATTERN 5

5.1   Intent

Assign instances of a dynamic principal entity to one and only one of a number of subtypes; model exclusive categories of a named group (noun).

5.2   Structure

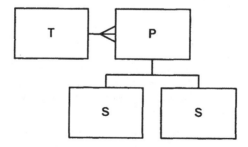

5.3 Discussion

This pattern models what is sometimes called an "exclusive type" association: an instance of P may be of (at most)[56] one type (category) or another, but it can be of only one: it can't change categories, even over time.

P has associated S entities if there is data that applies to one subcategory of instances of P, but not to others. There will be a minimum of two S entities in the pattern, but no maximum number.

The P table has the characteristics already defined: one originating unique primary key of one or more columns and at least one non-key attribute column. It will also have a column for the foreign key copied down from T.

P's association with its corresponding S entities is both identifying and categorizing: it copies down as each S's primary key. The PS association is mandatory-one-to-optional-one: an instance of P either is or is not an instance of a particular S. Note that P's primary key may be compound.

Each S table has at least two columns:

- One or more columns for its primary key, which is copied down from P
- One or more non-key attribute columns containing the data specific to the subtype.

In the simplest case the key columns are the same for each S. Some of the S tables may have some non-key attributes in common.[57] But not all: if a non-key attribute is common to *all* S entities, it is placed in P.

The instances of one S table are unique to that table: no other S contains any of those same instances.

T is always a parent entity. The T table has two or more columns:

---

[56] An instance of P may exist independent of any S. That is, it may have *no* category: it would be of "Type Zero." But this situation would usually be only temporary: a category would be assigned later in the data entry process.

[57] This does not, however, produce data redundancy. When a data item is input, it is stored in the appropriate S table, but in that table alone: if the instance is of type 1, the data item is stored only in the S1 table, etc.

- One for its single-part originating primary key
- One and only one non-key attribute column containing the names of the S entities and possibly the name of the P entity
- Other non-key attribute columns as necessary.

The names in T's name column must exactly match the names of the S entities and the P entity.

5.4 Collaboration, Sample

TPSS can be the entire physical database. Let's consider

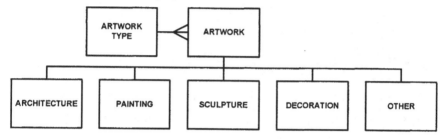

The T table identifies the S tables:

type id#	type_name
1	architecture
2	painting
3	sculpture
4	decoration
5	other

The P table holds the records of all the artworks, including the data that applies to them all, regardless of type:

artwork id#	type_id#	artwork_title	creation_ date	artwork_ classifier
1	2	Triptych of the Annunciation: The Prophet Isaiah	1430/35	altar, Old Testament
2	2	Jacob's Dream	1639	Old Testament
3	4	Sistine Chapel Vault	1508 - 1512	Old Testament, New Testament
4	5	Suspended Artifact	1993	
5	2	Horses in a Field	1649	animal
6	1	Holy Cross Chapel	1756-64	church
7	3	Pergamon Altar, East Frieze: Athena Group		classical, god

The S tables will hold records of artworks that are all of one type. The included data applies to that type of artwork. Here's the PAINTINGS table:

artwork_id#	accession_ number	material	height	width
1	2463 recto	oil on panel	964	320
2	1117	oil on linen	1650	2266
5		oil on linen	800	1000

Here's the SCULPTURE table:

artwork_id#	accession_ number	material	height	width	depth
3		marble	2000	4000	8

And here's the ARCHITECTURE table:

artwork_id#	view	period	comment
6	exterior	Baroque	Houses the Treasure of St Vitus Cathedral.

Notice that some non-key attributes appear in more than one table.

TPSS can be part of a larger structure. The P entity can also be part of a PP or PIP pattern—for example,

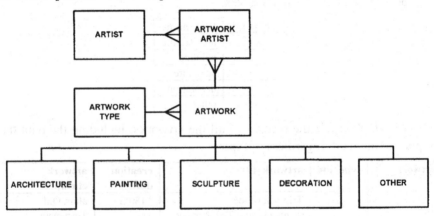

P may also be a mixed secondary/principal entity:

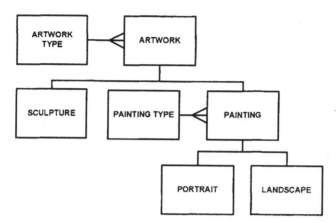

Here we have two TPSS patterns, with PAINTING serving as S to ARTWORK and as P to PORTRAIT and LANDSCAPE. The inheritance of keys is simple and obvious:

- artwork_type_no# is a foreign key in ARTWORK.
- artwork_id# is copied down from ARTWORK as the primary key for SCULPTURE, PAINTING, PORTRAIT, and LANDSCAPE.
- painting_type_no# is a foreign key in PAINTING.

5.5   Implementation

T is always a parent entity.

5.6   Closely Related Patterns

TRPSS, TPSSU

6.   NAME: TRPSS   PATTERN 6

6.1   Intent

Assign instances of a dynamic principal entity to one or more of a number of subtypes; model inclusive categories of a named group (noun).

6.2   Structure

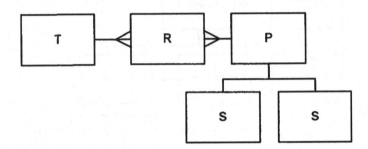

6.3   Discussion

This pattern models what is sometimes called an "inclusive type" association: an instance of P may be of more than one type (category) either from the outset or over time. That also means that an instance of T may apply, now or later, to zero, one, or many P instances.

P instances are connected to T instances in the R entity. The R entity is a special case of the I entity: it resolves the many-to-many association between T and P entities.

In most respects, the P, S, and T entities are the same as in the TPSS pattern:

1. P has associated S entities if there is data that applies to one subcategory of instances of P, but not to others. There will be a minimum of two S entities in the pattern, but no maximum number.
2. The P table has the characteristics already defined: one originating unique primary key of one or more columns and at least one non-key attribute column.
3. P's association with its corresponding S entities is both identifying and categorizing: it copies down as each S's primary key. The PS association is mandatory-one-to-optional-one: an instance of P either is or is not an instance of a particular S. Note that P's primary key may be compound.
4. Each S table has at least two columns:
   o   One or more columns for its primary key, which is copied down from P
   o   One or more non-key attribute columns containing the data specific to the subtype.

5. The key columns are the same for each S. Some of the S tables may have some non-key attributes in common. But not all: if a non-key attribute is common to all S entities, it is placed in P.
6. T is always a parent entity. The T table has two or more columns:
   o One for its single-part originating primary key
   o One and only one non-key attribute column containing the names of the S entities and possibly the name of the P entity
   o Other non-key attribute columns as necessary.
7. The names in T's name column must exactly match the names of the S entities.

Now for basic difference between TRPSS and TPSS: In contrast to its association in TPSS, in TRPSS the P entity does not receive a foreign key copied down from T. Instead, the primary keys of P and T copy down to R. Thus, the R table has at least two columns, one for each foreign key. The two foreign keys constitute R's compound primary key. Other columns in the R table might also exist. Their purpose would be to store information that describes the roles that instances of P can take.

If the P key and the T key do not together define a unique instance of R—that is, if a P instance has more than one role with respect to a particular category—a third component must be added to make R's primary key unique.

For example, consider the employee who can't decided whether to be exempt or not. If the T entity defines "exemptness" (that is, the S entities are "exempt" and "non-exempt"), the employee might be exempt for a time and non-exempt for a time, then exempt again. The addition of another part to R's key solves the problem.

P's association with R (P -|---|< R) is identifying, but not categorizing. The same is true for T's association with R. The TR association may be

- Mandatory-one-to-mandatory-many (each T instance must be associated with at least one R instance) *OR*
- Mandatory-one-to-optional-many (each T instance may have zero, one, or many associated R instances) *OR*
- Mandatory-one-to-optional-becoming-mandatory-many (each T instance must eventually have one or many associated R instances).

6.4 Collaboration, Implementation, Sample

TRPSS may constitute the entire physical database. Let's consider this example:

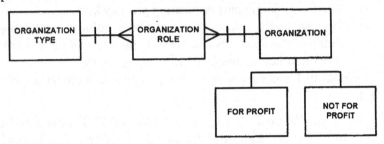

The ORGANIZATION table has columns like these:

organization_id#	organization_name
1	Kimball Services
2	Inmon Charities

The ORGANIZATION TYPE table has these two columns:

type_no#	type_description
1	for profit
2	not for profit

The ORGANIZATION ROLE table has four columns:

organization_id#	type_no#	from_date	through_date
1	1	03/06/2001	05/19/2003
1	2	5/20/2003	
2	2		

In this example, the organization changed from a for-profit to a not-for-profit about May 19, 2003.

6.5 Closely Related Patterns

TPSS

7. NAME: TPSSU   PATTERN 7

7.1 Intent

Associate instances of the same dynamic principal entity when each instance is, at the most, of one subtype; model recursion of exclusive instances of the same named group (noun).

7.2 Structure

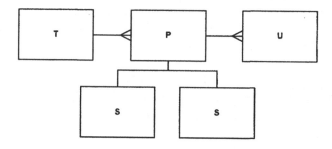

7.3 Discussion

Hierarchies—organization charts and bills of material, for example—sometimes include "exclusive type" associations: an instance of P will never be of more than one type (category), and an instance of T will apply, now or later, to zero, one, or many P instances.

P instances are connected to T instances directly: T's primary key is copied down to P and determines which S entity will receive which instance of P. In other words, T determines which subset of P instances is contained in which S entity

In most respects, the P, S, and T entities are the same as in the TPSS pattern:

1. P has associated S entities if there is data that applies to one subcategory of instances of P, but not to others. There will be a minimum of two S entities in the pattern, but no maximum number.
2. The P table has the characteristics already defined: one originating unique primary key of one or more columns and at least one non-key attribute column.

3. P's association with its corresponding S entities is both identifying and categorizing: its primary key copies down as each S's primary key. The PS association is mandatory-one-to-optional-one: an instance of P either is or is not an instance of a particular S. Note that P's primary key may be compound.

4. Each S table has at least two columns:
   o One or more columns for its primary key, which is copied down from P
   o One or more non-key attribute columns containing the data specific to the subtype.

5. The key columns are the same for each S. Some of the S tables may have some non-key attributes in common. But not all: if a non-key attribute is common to all S entities, it is placed in P.

6. T is always a parent entity. The T table has two or more columns:
   o One for its single-part originating primary key
   o One and only one non-key attribute column containing the names of the S entities and possibly the name of the P entity
   o Other non-key attribute columns as necessary.

7. The names in T's name column must exactly match the names of the S entities.

As in TPSS, P receives a foreign key copied down from T. T's association with P (T -|---|< P) is neither identifying nor categorizing. Thus, the foreign key that T is not part of P's primary key. Take, for example the case of an employee who is either a manager or a nonmanager, and who can never switch from one category to the other. The employee will be identified in the entity EMPLOYEE by a (usually) single-part primary key (e.g., employee_id#), and the foreign key (type_no#) will happily assign the employee to the appropriate S entity.

The TP association may be

- Mandatory-one-to-mandatory-many (each T instance must be associated with at least one P instance) *OR*
- Mandatory-one-to-optional-many (each T instance may have zero, one, or many associated P instances) *OR*
- Mandatory-one-to-optional-becoming-mandatory-many (each T instance must eventually have one or many associated P instances).

As for the other entities, it's business as usual. The primary key identifying the employee will be copied down to the S entity designated by T. The U entity will receive two copies of P's primary key for each relationship between two employees that must be recorded. One copy represents one employee, the other the other employee. Since P's association with U is identifying, the relationship between the two employees will be identified by a two-part primary key comprising the two foreign keys copied down from P.

7.4 Collaboration, Implementation, Sample

TPSSU can be the entire physical database, though such a relatively elaborate pattern is more likely to occur in large modeling projects and thus have connections to other patterns.

Let's look at a business that is organized in a hierarchy. It has

- a President (on the management payroll) who manages
- many Vice Presidents (on the management payroll), who in turn manage
- many workers (on the nonmanagement payroll).

It's an awfully strict hierarchy: A manager can never become a nonmanager, and a nonmanager can never become a manager.

We'll model the business this way:

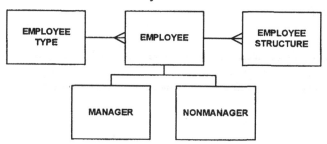

The EMPLOYEE TYPE (T) table has two columns:

type no#	type_description
1	manager
2	nonmanager

The EMPLOYEE (P) table has at least two columns:

employee id#	type_no#	title
1	1	President
2	1	VP Administration
3	1	VP Operations
4	2	clerk
5	2	welder

The MANAGER (S) table has at least two columns:

employee_id#	annual_salary
1	300000
2	200000
3	200000

The NONMANAGER (S) table has at least two columns with these headings:

employee_id#	hourly_wage
4	6.50
5	22.00

The EMPLOYEE STRUCTURE (U) table shows who manages whom:

employee_id# parent	employee_id# child
1	2
1	3
2	4
3	5

7.5   Closely Related Patterns

PU, TPSS

8.   NAME: TRUPSS   PATTERN 8

8.1   Intent

Associate instances of the same dynamic principal entity when each instance is of zero, one, or many subtypes; model recursion of inclusive instances of the same named group (noun).

8.2   Structure

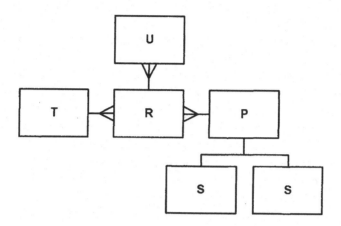

8.3   Discussion

As in TRPSS, this pattern models an "inclusive type" association: an instance of P may be of more than one type (category), and an instance of T may apply, now or later, to zero, one, or many P instances. As in TPSSU, the U entity relates different instances of the P entity. But TRUPSS has one major difference from both: the U entity relates different P instances *in their different roles*.

P instances are connected to T instances in the R entity. The R entity is a special case of the I entity: it resolves the many-to-many association between T and P entities.

In most respects, the P, S, T, and R entities are the same as in the TRPSS pattern:

1. P has associated S entities if there is data that applies to one subcategory of instances of P, but not to others. There will be a minimum of two S entities in the pattern, but no maximum number.
2. The P table has the characteristics already defined: one originating unique primary key of one or more columns and at least one non-key attribute column.
3. P's association with its corresponding S entities is both identifying and categorizing: its key copies down as each S's primary key. The PS association is mandatory-one-to-optional-one: an instance of P either is or is not an instance of a particular S. Note that P's primary key may be compound.

4. Each S table has at least two columns:
   o One or more columns for its primary key, which is copied down from P
   o One or more non-key attribute columns containing the data specific to the subtype.
5. The key columns are the same for each S. Some of the S tables may have some non-key attributes in common. But not all: if a non-key attribute is common to all S entities, it is placed in P.
6. T is always a parent entity. The T table has two or more columns:
   o One for its single-part originating primary key
   o One and only one non-key attribute column containing the names of the S entities and possibly the name of the P entity
   o Other non-key attribute columns as necessary.
7. The names in T's name column must exactly match the names of the S entities and possibly the name of the P entity.
8. T and P are both parent entities to R. P's association with R (P -|---|< R) is identifying, but not categorizing. The same is true for T's association with R. The primary keys of P and T copy down to R and together constitute R's primary key. The R table has at least two columns:
   o One for each foreign key
   o One or more non-key attribute columns containing relevant information such as the name or a description of the role.
9. If the P key and the T key do not together define a unique instance of R—that is, if a P instance has more than one role with respect to a particular S category—a third component must be added to make R's primary key unique.
10. The TR association may be
   o Mandatory-one-to-mandatory-many (each T instance must be associated with at least one R instance) *OR*
   o Mandatory-one-to-optional-many (each T instance may have zero, one, or many associated R instances) *OR*
   o Mandatory-one-to-optional-becoming-mandatory-many (each T instance must eventually have one or many associated R instances).

What is new with TRUPSS is the RU association. R has a compound primary key of two or more parts. The function of the U entity is to relate two instances of R, so R's compound primary key copies down twice to the U entity. Thus, U has a compound primary key of at least four parts:

key_no# (1), type_no# (1), key_no# (2), type_no# (2).

The two <u>key no#</u> foreign keys originate in P, and the <u>type no#</u> keys originate, of course, in T.

Notice one interesting thing, though: the <u>key no#</u> foreign keys may refer to the same instance of P, as long as the associated keys <u>type no#</u> (1) and <u>type no#</u> (2) are different. For example, an instance of U may relate English Paper Products in its role as customer to English Paper Products in its role as supplier. In U, we'd have an instance like this: <u>key no#</u> (1), <u>type no#</u> (1), <u>key no#</u> (1), <u>type no#</u> (2).

Likewise, two different instances of P can be related to each other even though they are of the same type: English Paper Products as a customer can be related to Graziano Paints as a customer. U would have an instance like this: <u>key no#</u> (1), <u>type no#</u> (1), <u>key no#</u> (2), <u>type no#</u> (1).

Presumably, English Paper Products as customer could even be related to itself in that same category, English Paper Products as customer. If there is a need, the U entity can accommodate such an instance. If, however, the interest is in the role alone, in English Paper Products as a customer, the information is stored in the R table.

8.4 Collaboration, Implementation, Sample

TRUPSS may constitute the entire physical database, though that is unlikely. Let's look at a specialized example:

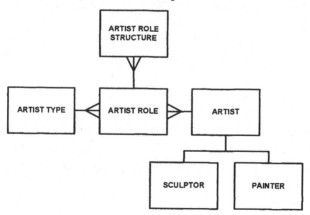

The purpose of this database is to track collaborations between artists, some of whom are painters and some of whom are sculptors.[58]

The ARTIST table has columns like these:

artist_id#	artist_name
1	Hans von Kulmbach
2	Tilman Riemanschneider
3	Claes Oldenburg
4	Donald Judd

The ARTIST TYPE table has these two columns:

type_no#	type_description
1	sculptor
2	painter

The ARTIST ROLE table has columns like these:

artist_id#	type_no#	role_comment
1	1	Master of Public Works
1	2	Member, Guild of St Luke
2	1	Master carver in limewood
3	1	Presented "found objects" as sculpture
3	2	Associated with Pop Art movement
4	2	Associated with Pop Art movement

The ARTIST ROLE STRUCTURE table has columns like these:

artist_id# (1)	type_no# (1)	artist_id# (2)	type_no# (2)	from_date
1	1	2	1	1545
1	2	2	1	1537
3	1	3	2	1968

We're being told here that

- Hans von Kulmbach and Tilman Riemanschneider worked together as sculptors from 1545.
- Hans von Kulmbach worked alongside Tilman Riemanschneider, the one as a painter and the other as a sculptor, from the year 1537.
- Claes Oldenburg worked both as a painter and a sculptor from 1968 onward.

---

[58] This is just an example. Don't trust it as art history.

A freestanding database of this sort is pretty limited in its usefulness. It needs to be integrated into a database of larger scope, one including entities like LOCATION.

8.5   Closely Related Patterns

TRPSS, TPSSU

Chapter 12

FROM LOGICAL TO PHYSICAL

Wherein we prepare to make dreams come true

1. REVISE, REVISE, REVISE ... AND FINALIZE

Ideally, enterprise data modeling is a continuous process. After all, change is constant: the economy changes, the competition changes, new regulations and standards come into effect, and the result is change in your business. But fact is, you've been doing process/operational modeling, aimed toward automating functions in your department. That means you have a project deadline to meet. For the short term and immediate purposes, you've got to come to a conclusion.

So. You have completed your logical data model. All the *I*s are dotted, all the *T*s crossed. Now's the time to perform a final check.

Let's walk down a basic checklist.

1. If you've used an automated tool to build your model, use it again to **check for obvious errors**. With some tools you can set the level of sensitivity for error checking, so it can seek out problems of varying degrees of seriousness. Set the tool to find anything and everything that could possibly cause a problem, and run the diagnosis. When error and warning messages appear, some will be very familiar and will not represent real problems. But you may find something you missed earlier. Do whatever is necessary to make the model consistent with itself: the cost of finding and fixing an error will only grow as development progresses.

2. **Check your model against the business statements.** Using the Statement-Entity matrix, check to ensure that all business statements are consistent with each other, that no business statements are missing, and that you have not created business statements out of thin air. Your goal is to ensure that the problem is stated correctly and that you are solving the right problem. Check also to ensure that every row and every column in the Statement-Entity matrix has at least one check mark and that no row or column is too heavily populated with check marks.

3. **Check your data map against the eight design patterns.** The patterns show how entities are put together; they help you do the job quickly, cheaply, and accurately. Check to make sure that every pair of entities fits a design pattern. Take time to check (1) cardinality, (2) optionality, and (3) how the primary keys copy down from parent entities to child entities.

4. **Make sure your entity associations make real-world sense.** Make complete sentences out of each entity pair. In the case of role and intersecting entities, you'll have to consider three entities at a time, and structure entities talk to themselves. Get together with the other subject matter experts, and read your sentences out loud to them. If your project methodology uses walkthroughs (Yourdon 1989: 515-521), conduct a walkthrough with the subject matter experts and the database people. This is an excellent way to get these groups to start communicating, and this is the right time to do it.

5. Now we get down to details:
   o   Are all many-to-many associations properly resolved?
   o   Are all associations valid?
   o   Are all key structures correct?
   o   Does every secondary entity have at least one mate?
   o   Does each entity have at least two attribute columns? And is at least one column used for all or part of the primary key?
   o   Is a domain specified for each attribute?
   o   Is a length (and possibly a precision) specified for each attribute that requires one?
   o   If you've defined the key attribute's domain (and length, if necessary) in a parent entity, does the corresponding key in the child entity have compatible characteristic(s)?

2. ESTABLISHING REFERENTIAL INTEGRITY

You're approaching the point when your logical data model must be translated into the tables of a **physical database** realized in a **database management system (DBMS)**. But first, some heavy lifting. To keep your physical database consistent with itself, you will probably want to enforce **referential integrity**. All we mean by referential integrity is this:

If we have an association between row A in the parent table and rows B, C, etc., in the child table, what do we need to do to maintain consistency between rows A and rows B and C and beyond?

According to the logical data model, the parent's primary key is passed to the child as a foreign key. In the physical database, whenever a row is added, updated, or deleted in the parent table, constraints—for example, a *foreign key constraint*—are applied. These constraints define what changes are subsequently permitted in the child table. Can rows be added? Can they be deleted? Can they be changed? And how?

Similar constraints limit changes to the parent table when the child table is changed. For example, if every row in the parent table must have at least one corresponding row in the child table, what happens when row B in the child table is deleted? Logically, the DBMS would

1. find the corresponding row (row A) in the parent table,
2. find out if any other rows in the child table correspond to row A,
3. if other such rows exist, take no action, OR
4. if no other such rows exist, delete row A.

But sometimes, our business statements may be ambiguous about referential integrity, or enforcement of referential integrity may not even be desirable. For example, in data warehouses vast quantities of data are often inserted into huge tables in bulk. If referential integrity is turned on, performance can be impossibly slow. But if referential integrity is turned off, all insertions can usually be completed in a fraction of the time that would otherwise be required.

Referential integrity is a feature provided by many (but not all) database engines, and a valuable feature it is. If your **Database Administrator (DBA)** builds referential integrity into the physical database, your developers will not have to spend their time enforcing referential integrity in code. Instead, they can capture and compensate for the errors produced when a user attempts to violate an integrity constraint. They may even develop or implement application features that keep users from attempting to violate referential integrity in the first place.

2.1 Referential integrity at work

Let's look at an example. Here's a familiar TPSS pattern:

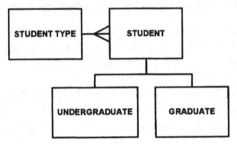

Now let's imagine the corresponding physical database tables (simplified, of course):

T	STUDENT TYPE	
	1	Undergraduate
	2	Graduate

P	STUDENT	
	1	Fred Smith
	2	Virginia Jones

S	UNDERGRADUATE	
	1	3.44

S	GRADUATE	
	1	University of Wyoming

In the UNDERGRADUATE table we store grade point averages for undergraduate students. In the GRADUATE table we store the name of the graduate student's undergraduate degree granting institution.

Let's focus on the association between the STUDENT table and the UNDERGRADUATE table:

STUDENT -|---o- UNDERGRADUATE

We are going to consider what we want to have happen when an insertion, a deletion, or an update occurs. (The database does not change when we merely *read* the contents of a row.) To do this, we need to look at each action from both sides of the association: what happens when we insert, delete, or update on the parent table, and what happens when we do the same on the child table. Here are the cases we'll consider:

	Insertion	**Deletion**	**Update**
Parent	Case 1	Case 3	Case 5
Child	Case 2	Case 4	Case 6

We want to come up with procedures for imposing our will on these tables. And here's our analysis.

Case 1: Parent table row insertion

A new row is to be inserted into the STUDENT table. We don't yet want to insert a corresponding row or rows into the UNDERGRADUATE table—perhaps because we don't yet know whether the student will be enrolling as an undergraduate or as a graduate student.

Ruling: Allowed by our business statements and by the PS association, which does not require an instance of P to have a subtype. Thus, no corresponding (optional) row is required in the UNDERGRADUATE table.

Case 2: Child table row insertion

A new row is to be inserted into the UNDERGRADUATE table. We don't yet want to insert a corresponding row into the STUDENT table.

Ruling: Not allowed by our business statements and the nature of the PS association: if an undergraduate exists, he or she has to be registered as a student. Thus a corresponding (mandatory) row is required in the STUDENT table.

Solution: Insert a row into the STUDENT table, and then insert the corresponding row into the UNDERGRADUATE table.

Case 3: Parent table row deletion

An existing row is to be deleted from the STUDENT table. We don't yet want to delete the corresponding rows from the UNDERGRADUATE table.

Ruling: Not allowed according to our business statements and the nature of the PS association. A row in the UNDERGRADUATE table demands a corresponding (mandatory) row in the STUDENT table.

Solution: Delete the corresponding rows from the UNDERGRADUATE table, and then delete the row from the STUDENT table

Case 4: Child table row deletion

An existing row is to be deleted from the UNDERGRADUATE table. We don't yet want to delete the corresponding row from the STUDENT table.

Ruling: Allowed according to our business statements and the nature of the PS association. A row in the STUDENT table does not demand a corresponding (optional) row in the UNDERGRADUATE table.

Case 5: Parent table row update

The key value for an existing row in the STUDENT table is to be changed, perhaps from "1" to "1564". We don't yet want to update the corresponding row or rows in the UNDERGRADUATE table.

Ruling: Not allowed according to our business statements and the nature of the PS association. A row in the UNDERGRADUATE table demands a corresponding (mandatory) row in the STUDENT table.

Solution: Insert a new row into the STUDENT table with the key value "1564". Update the corresponding row in the UNDERGRADUATE table with the new key value. Delete the old row in the STUDENT table that has the key value of "1".

Case 6: Child table row update

The key value for an existing row in the UNDERGRADUATE table is to be changed, perhaps from "1" to "1564". We don't yet want to delete the corresponding row in the STUDENT table.

Ruling: Not allowed according to our business statements and the nature of the PS association. A row in the STUDENT table still does not demand a corresponding row in the UNDERGRADUATE table. However, if a corresponding row *does* exist in the UNDERGRADUATE table, that row must have a key which exists in a (mandatory) row in the STUDENT table.

Solution: Insert a new row into the STUDENT table with the value "1564". Update the corresponding row in the UNDERGRADUATE table with the new key value. Delete the row in the STUDENT table with the value of "1".

2.2 Referential integrity in general

So much for the STUDENT -|---o- UNDERGRADUATE association. Now let's return to referential integrity in general, so that we can apply it to any kind of valid association. IBM defines referential integrity this way:

> Referential integrity is the state of a database in which all values of all foreign keys are valid. Each value of the foreign key must also exist in the parent key or be null. (IBM, iSeries Information Center)

Referential integrity applies to associations, and each association may have zero or more of what are called **referential constraints**. Each referential constraint simply says what actions are allowed and what actions are not allowed when referential integrity is invoked. Different constraints are invoked at different times in the process of executing commands to make changes to the database.

Sometimes, more than one referential constraint applies to an association, or multiple referential constraints may be involved—as, for example, when deleting a row in a child table of a child table. In such cases, the order of execution must be considered.

The DBA will know ways of getting things done with or without the use of referential integrity. The DBA uses English-like phrases (e.g. ON UPDATE NO ACTION) to tell the database engine how to build referential integrity into an association.

To see how this might be done, let's look at each kind of action (insert, delete, update) in turn. Our discussion won't be exhaustive, and you should be aware that different database engines implement referential integrity in different ways.

2.2.1 Insertion

Recall the rule we set out in Chapter 5, that every association must have exactly one strong mandatory side. We call this the "strong mandatory 'one'" rule. When referential integrity is invoked, this rule means that every row in a child table must have a foreign key value linking it to a corresponding row in a parent table. Thus, the row in the parent table must exist before any corresponding row can be inserted into the child table.

2.2.2 Deletion

IBM DB2 recognizes four choices when performing a deletion with referential integrity: NO ACTION, RESTRICT, CASCADE, and SET NULL. If you attempt to delete a row from a parent table, one of these four constraints will apply.

If we try to delete a row from a parent table and ON DELETE NO ACTION or ON DELETE RESTRICT is specified, DB2 will check all child tables for corresponding rows. If even one corresponding child row exists, the operation fails. That's because the "strong mandatory 'one'" rule requires that a row in a child table have a corresponding row in a parent table. We can't delete the row from the parent table and leave a row in a child table with no parent.

If ON DELETE CASCADE is specified for the parent table, deleting a row from the parent table will result in deletion of all corresponding rows in the child table. That way, there are no orphaned rows in the child table. Referential integrity is enforced and the database is in a consistent state. But we need to be sure we really wanted to lose the data in the child table.

If we delete a row in the parent table and ON DELETE SET NULL is specified, DB2 finds all the corresponding rows in the child table, finds the foreign keys inherited from the deleted row, and sets all those foreign keys to a value of null. All connection with any row in the parent table is lost, but the rows in the child table, and their precious data, remain. Of course, this is inconsistent with the "strong mandatory 'one'" rule.

Our point is this: the "strong mandatory 'one'" rule builds referential integrity into the logical data model. Our resulting physical database is thus less likely to have orphaned rows in child tables, rows that lack corresponding rows in parent tables. And once constructed, our database is likely to be in (and stay in) a consistent state: all rows in all tables are present and accounted for. You will need to work with the DBA to define appropriate referential integrity.

2.2.3 Update

For performing an update with referential integrity, IBM DB2 recognizes two choices: NO ACTION and RESTRICT. The difference between these choices is subtle, but each works to ensure that the database remains in a consistent state. The way IBM explains it,

"The update rule of a referential constraint is specified when the referential constraint is defined. The choices are NO ACTION and RESTRICT. The update rule applies when a row of the parent or a row of the dependent table is updated.

"In the case of a parent row, when a value in a column of the parent key is updated:

- if any row in the dependent table matched the original value of the key, the update is rejected when the update rule is RESTRICT
- if any row in the dependent table does not have a corresponding parent key when the update statement is completed (excluding AFTER triggers), the update is rejected when the update rule is NO ACTION.

"In the case of a dependent row, the update rule that is implicit when a foreign key is specified is NO ACTION. NO ACTION means that a non-null update value of a foreign key must match some value of the parent key of the parent table when the update statement is completed.

"The value of a composite foreign key is null if any component of the value is null." (IBM DB2 Technical Support)

2.2.4 CRUD

CRUD stands for "Create, Read, Update, and Delete." These are the only four operations that can be performed on one or more rows in a database table.

We can use **CRUD matrices** to specify

1. Which individuals have authority to access which tables in a database, and what operations those individuals are allowed to perform
2. Which business processes need to access which tables in a database, and what operations can be performed on their behalf
3. Which screens and reports require access to which tables in a database, and what operations they can perform.

A CRUD matrix can often communicate a great deal of information in a small space. Consider the following CRUD matrix, generated using Visible Advantage:

Entities / Processes	ADDRESS	APPLICANT	EMPLOYEE	EXEMPT EMPLOYEE	INTERNAL ORGANIZATION	JOB	JOB SKILL	NON EXEMPT EMPLOYEE
Add Employee		c	cr	cr		r		cr
Add Person Address	cr	c	cr	cr				cr
Add Person Skill								
Create ADDRESS	c							
Create APPLICANT		c	cr	cr				cr
Create EMPLOYEE		c	cr	cr				cr
Create EXEMPT EMPLOYEE		c	cr	cr				cr
Create INTERNAL ORGANIZATION					cr	c		
Create JOB					r	c		
Create JOB SKILL						r	c	
Create NON EXEMPT EMPLOYEE		c	cr	cr				cr
Create ORGANIZATION					cr	c		

This CRUD matrix is of the second type, linking business processes with entities. It details which business processes create and read rows in each table. Of course, a more complete CRUD matrix would show processes for updating rows in and even deleting rows from tables. Your DBA should be very familiar with CRUD matrices, and you will find that they contribute substantially to communication.

3.   PREPARING FOR THE DATABASE PEOPLE

When you've finished all this checking, you can say that you have answered the "What" question: you've defined what the business people want to do with the database that is to be built. The purely logical work is done, at least until someone changes a business statement. Now it's up to you to prepare to talk to the database people in heavy-duty database terms and to the developers who will write or implement the user interface.

Be aware that business people and technical people use different vocabularies. While we have used the words "entity," "attribute," and "association," for example, database people are much more likely to express themselves in the corresponding physical terms: "table," "column," and "join."

Your immediate task is to **convert your logical data model into a physical database.** If a suitable automated tool is available, use it to automatically copy the logical data model from the tool's logical side to its physical side. Using the facilities of the tool's physical side, you'll find that (1) many of the required conversions have been accomplished automatically and (2) the tool makes many of the remaining conversions easy.

Here, then, are the conversions you need to make:

1. Convert each logical entity into a physical table. The table may be split into parts later, or it may be combined with another table or tables. Worry about splits and merges later.
2. Convert each logical attribute into a physical column. Again, mergers and splits may occur later.
3. Convert the domain for each logical attribute into a corresponding physical data type, complete with length and precision where required. Remember: different database systems have different physical data types, as well as different implementations of common types. Dates and times can usually be specified in different formats: you'll need to specify what works for your particular problem. Your organization may provide a standard for you to follow.
4. Ensure that all table names and column names are compatible with the database engine you plan to use. Pay attention to length limits. DB2 UDB, for example, limits names to 18 characters unless the DBA specifies a different value.
5. Convert all logical "mandatory-one-to-optional-becoming-many" (-|---o|<) associations to physical "mandatory-one-to-optional-many" (-|---o<) **joins**[59].

---

[59] A join is a DBMS operation that takes data from two or more tables and combines them to create a virtual table that is optimized for a particular purpose. A join occurs when data are inserted into, read from, updated in, or deleted from the tables at the same time.

6. Convert all logical "mandatory-one-to-optional-becoming-one" (-|---o|-) associations to physical "mandatory-one-to-optional-one" (-|---o-) joins.

4.   MORE HEAVY LIFTING

Several other tasks remain before our data model is ready to become a database. The DBA is the person best qualified to undertake them.

1. Our logical data model used identifying associations to define the compound keys for R, I, and U entities. But when it comes to building the physical database, the DBA may have to convert some of those associations to non-identifying associations, reducing the number of parts to the primary key. One benefit of this change might be to reduce the number of joins required for an operation against the database. A one-column key may offer much better performance than a five-column key.

2. Type entities might be expressed in some other form, perhaps as check constraints (showing, for example, a list of valid values), eliminating the need for a table (and consequently eliminating the need for a join).

The DBA will also be very interested in activities which we haven't begun to explore:

- Estimating table size, index size, query activity, growth, transaction volume, access path volume, and other measurable aspects of the physical database
- Planning indexes for key attributes, candidate keys, selection attributes, and any other attributes on which queries will normally be run
- Defining "views"—windows into the database—to make development easier and to allow for improvements in security
- Defining locks: what should happen when two users attempt to change the same row in the same table at the same time?
- Planning and optimizing queries
- Optimizing physical storage.

And of course, when push comes to shove, your DBA will have to deal with issues like these:

- What database engine you're going to use: e.g. DB2 UDB for the AS/400, DB2 UDB under OS/390, Microsoft SQL Server under Windows 2000, or any one or more of dozens of other products
- Where you (or the technical people) want the actual database or parts of the database to reside: e.g., in Boston or Los Angeles, on the fast server or the slow server, or even with different parts of the same database in different locations
- Whether your business operations will be adding and updating data (inserting rows) more frequently (or less frequently) than they will be reading rows to generate printed reports
- Whether anyone expects to tap the database for goodies: extract data, transform it in various ways, and load the transformed data into another file structure, such as an operational data store or a data mart
- What indexing, backup, and other options are needed and whether they're available (or can be acquired for a slight additional charge) for the target database engine
- Whether the database engine employs cost-based optimization or rules-based optimization in planning execution of SQL (Structured Query Language) statements.

You may not know how to answer many of these questions. Some may not even make much sense right now. The Database Administrator is responsible for answering them, and you need to make yourself available when he has questions. From this point on, the DBA is the most important friend you've got, the person responsible for your database and its associated applications, the person who knows from experience what works and what doesn't work and where to get answers. Get the DBA on your side and keep him there.

By the time he has finished all his estimating, planning, defining, and optimizing, your DBA should have a very good idea of how he will actually construct the physical database. He will almost certainly want to denormalize some of the structures you spent so much time normalizing.

5. DENORMALIZATION

Recall that when we normalized, we gave every non-key attribute a home in exactly one entity. Each non-key attribute was entirely dependent on the key, the whole key, and nothing but the key. In contrast to normalization, denormalization takes what used to be normalized entities and moves their attributes around in various ways.

You may ask, "Why would anyone denormalize a normalized database?" The usual answer is "To improve performance." For instance, retrieving data from a fully normalized database is often slow, because related data items must be retrieved simultaneously from more than one table using one or more joins. Joins are expensive in terms of computing performance. Reduce the number of joins, and you improve performance. Denormalize, and you reduce the number of joins.

Of course, we don't want to denormalize if we don't have to. In his outstanding book on database administration, Craig Mullins acknowledges "the simple rule of creating a table for each entity in the logical data model," and he advises that "The only reason to deviate ... is if application performance or data availability would be unacceptable without a change."[60]

So what should we do if our physical database isn't up to snuff? Mr. Mullins recommends several very well defined types of denormalization and establishes the situations in which they should be used (2002: 141-151). While the work of denormalization is best left to your DBA, this discussion should help you to understand what he is doing and why he is doing it.

Let's consider ten different problems.

Problem 1: Two or more tables must be joined regularly, but the cost of repeatedly joining the tables is high.

Solution: Create **prejoined tables**.

How: Join the tables once and store and reuse the result, rather than executing the join repeatedly. This creates redundant data and a need for extra management.

Example: We have a logical TPSS pattern normalized to Third normal form. Instead of creating four or more physical tables, we create a single table, with the columns from the secondary and type entities rolled into the dynamic P table. Of course, a lot of null values will have to be created: rows representing subtype A will not have values for the attributes associated with subtype B, and vice versa. But the single table has fewer joins, and as we've said, joins are expensive.

---

[60] Mullins 2002: 122; see also Chapter 4: Database Design (121-158).

Problem 2: An end user report requires formatting or data manipulation that SQL cannot provide.

Solution: Create a **report table**.

How: Prepare a table with one column for each report element, physically sequenced to eliminate sorting. The report table contains data that already exists elsewhere in the database. So, once again, we have redundant data requiring management. But the table can be populated once, then maintained only as necessary, and the report is much easier and faster to generate.

Problem 3: An active application system has some users querying the database and other users modifying the same database at the same time. A resource conflict exists, because insertions and reads are being attempted simultaneously on the same physical database.

Solution: Create **mirror tables**.

How: Create a set of tables in the foreground for application processing (updates) and a different set of tables in the background for decision support (reads). The background tables will be updated only at intervals (for example, in the case of a data warehouse), and not in real time

Problem 4: Separate pieces of one normalized table are accessed by distinct groups of users with little or no overlap.

Solution: Create **split tables**.

How: Split the table, either horizontally or vertically. For example, if geography (distributed access) is an issue, one logical table could be divided like so: the top physical half of the rows could be placed on a server in Boston, while the bottom physical half could reside on a server in Los Angeles. Each half is determined by a range of key values: rows with a key value less than X go to Boston, and the rest go to Los Angeles.

Then again, a vertical split might be more appropriate if, say, corporate management resides in Boston and the publications division is in Los Angeles. The vertical split could divide the logical table so that text and numbers are in one physical half and CLOBs (Character Large Objects) are in the other. Rows in each portion of the table would be kept in sync by repeating the same key values: each row in Boston has the same key value as its partner in Los Angeles.

Problem 5: Two tables are associated in a one-to-one relationship.

Solution: Combine the tables into a single table.

How: Just do it. This is a good idea for those situations in which the logical data modeler erred. (Remember: -|---|- associations should be avoided.) However, combining physical tables may not always be a good idea. For instance, when fixed length data and LOBs (Large Objects) exist in the same logical row, the physical characteristics of LOBs may demand treatment different from the treatment that fixed length data requires.

Problem 6: Almost every time that data in one table is accessed, a column or columns from a second table are accessed.

Solution: Create redundant data.

How: Repeat the data from the second table in the first table. This reduces the penalty for repeated joins, but it also increases the difficulties of managing the database. After all, changes to the data in the second table will have to be migrated to the first table. Whether this is done in real time or by batch will be affected by factors such as how critical the data is and how often it changes.

Problem 7: Repeating groups of data are regularly retrieved.

Solution: Structure the table to hold repeating groups.

How: The repeating groups are stored as cells in the same row of a table. Create extra columns in a table and populate them with the repeating group data. Of course, this solution violates even the First normal form rule.

Problem 8: Repeated calculation of derived data is prohibitively expensive.

Solution: Store derived data.

How: Derive the data once and store it in a column.

Example: Consider your checking account. If the bank's database were normalized to Third normal form, your bank would have to recompute your balance, starting from the time you opened the account, every time you made a balance inquiry and whenever your monthly statement appeared. Obviously, this activity can be fraught with error, and it is expensive. By deriving and storing data, we reduce expense.

Problem 9: Data represent a hierarchy, such as a parts explosion (for a manufacturing firm) or an organization chart. This is the situation we addressed earlier with the Structure entity: each instance relates a part, for instance, to one of its components—which is, of course, another part.

Solution: Create a **speed table**.

How: Generate a table that represents a pretraversed hierarchy. Each physical speed table, corresponding to our logical structure entity, has a two-part primary key. In addition, the speed table contains two columns not found in the structure entity. The first column shows the number of levels in the hierarchy intervening between the item identified by the parent primary key and the item identified by the child primary key. The second added column specifies whether the item identified by the child primary key is at the bottom of the hierarchy.

For example, here are columns that a speed table for a parts explosion might have:

PART HIERARCHY		(table name)
	Parent part number	(key column)
	Child part number	(key column)
	Level number	(number of levels between parent and child)
	Bottom level	(yes or no)

So much for columns. In addition–and this is the "pretraversed" part–the table has a row for each item at any level of the hierarchy *which is in a hierarchical relationship with another item.* If two items, at the same or different levels, do not have a hierarchical association with each other, no such row exists. If we have a large number of related items in our hierarchy, we will have a table with a great many rows.

Let's look at another example. A university has list of all employees, given in table form below. For brevity, we assume that no other individuals are employees.

Key	Title	Person Name
1	President	Able
2	VP of Academics	Baker
3	VP of Research	Charlie
4	Dean of Animal Science	Delta
5	Dean of Plant Sciences	Echo
6	Professor of Plant Sciences	Foxtrot
7	Associate VP Patents	Golf

This is a properly normalized table, but the speed table on the many side of the -|---o< relationship is not.

The speed table needs to show that Dr. Baker and Dr. Charlie report directly to President Able, that Dean Delta and Dean Echo report directly to Vice President Baker, that Professor Foxtrot reports directly to Dean Echo, and that Dr. Golf reports directly to Dr. Charlie.

In addition, it needs to show multilevel relationships with a level distance greater than 1: Deans Delta and Echo reporting (though not directly) to President Able; Professor Foxtrot reporting to President Able, Dr. Baker, and Dean Echo; and Dr. Golf reporting to President Able. Each of these pairs involves at least three levels in the hierarchy (remember, these are not direct reports).

Here's what the speed table might look like: The "Parent" key shows who is higher in the hierarchy. The "Child" key shows who is lower in the hierarchy. The Level column shows the number of levels between the entry in the "Parent" column and the entry in the "Child" column. The "Lowest" column contains "Y" if the entry in the "Child" key column is at the bottom of the hierarchy (nobody is reporting to the person identified by the "Child" key) and "N" if the person identified by the "Child" key has subordinates.

Parent	Child	Level	Lowest
1	2	1	N
1	3	1	N
1	4	2	Y
1	5	2	N
1	6	3	Y
1	7	2	Y
2	4	1	Y
2	5	1	N
2	6	2	Y
3	7	1	Y
5	6	1	Y

If we tried querying our hierarchy without having a speed table, we'd get an inefficient and time consuming mess: the query would be many lines long and take a long time to run, chewing up computer resources better used elsewhere. Depending on the number of layers in the hierarchy, the query could become overwhelmingly complex.

Problem 10: The database management system's physical limitations adversely affect performance.

Solution: Other denormalization.

How: Denormalize the data as required to fit the limitation.

Example: DB2 has explicit rules about the relative sequence of variable length and fixed length data in a row. The DBA knows how to apply these rules to their best effect.

6.   DATA DEFINITION LANGUAGE (DDL)

So now we've covered referential integrity, CRUD, denormalization, and various other solutions to issues and problems that occur when the logical data model has to be converted into the design for a physical database. The DBA has most of the responsibility for applying these solutions to your database-to-be. Once that's done, it's time to create the database in the database management system using Data Definition Language (DDL).

DDL is a subset of SQL (Structured Query Language) used for defining the structure of a relational database to a **database engine**, which then proceeds to build the physical database. Once the physical considerations identified above have been treated, DDL statements specific to a database engine can be written by hand or generated by many software engineering tools. A parser within the target database engine parses the DDL and generates tables, columns, joins, and other physical database objects.

Most of the time, the DBA uses a tool to generate the DLL script. Then he checks the script carefully:

1. Vital aspects of the database may not be supported by the tool. For example, the tool might not permit specification of necessary index types (e.g., reverse key indexes or partitioned indexes) or referential integrity strategies (e.g., ON DELETE CASCADE), even when the target database management system offers full support.
2. The tool's error checking apparatus may not catch interesting errors. For example, the tool might fail to report any errors whatsoever when all associations in the logical data model are specified as identifying.
3. The tool's DDL generating facility may generate faulty DDL.
4. Because a physical table can be a parent to a child physical table, the CREATE TABLE statement for the parent table must appear in the DDL script prior to the CREATE TABLE statement for the child table. Among other things, this means that foreign key constraints generally become more frequent as the DDL generation progresses. Each FOREIGN KEY constraint (and every other constraint) must be checked.
5. The length in characters (bytes) of database object names (tables, constraints, and so on) may be greater than the length in characters permitted by the database management system.

The generated DDL can be used for purposes other than just building physical databases.

- Reverse engineering has been possible for years. DDL can be imported into many tools and converted automatically to Class Diagrams as defined within the Unified Modeling Language (Booch *et al.* 1999). These Class Diagrams can be modified and used to generate code in any number of object oriented languages.
- Reingruber and Gregory (1994: 41-44) and Finkelstein (1992: 424-437) use logical data maps to partition out clusters of closely related entities which can be considered units of work. Their process can also be used with the corresponding physical tables.

7. NEW NOTIONS

Physical database, referential integrity, database management system (DBMS), Database Administrator (DBA), referential constraint, foreign key constraint, CRUD, CRUD matrix, denormalization, Structured Query Language (SQL), join, prejoined tables, report table, mirror tables, split tables, speed table, Data Definition Language (DDL), database engine, Unified Modeling Language

Chapter 13

THE END AND THE BEGINNING

Wherein we see the rewards of virtue

It's been a good day, your first day as the new General Manager of Pinebeach Screen Printing and Embroidery. The job isn't easy, but without the new system it would be a real bear.

The new system. New, custom-made system. New, custom-made, computer-based work order—there's that term again. Funny how it no longer makes you shudder. A new work order management system. For tracking work orders and customers. Installed last Saturday.

When the owner promoted you, he made it clear why:

"What you've done here really simplifies our life. Used to be, it would take three to five hours a day to compile orders. Now, five minutes and the job's done. I mean, we're really pleased with it. It's very exciting, what you've done. You should be real proud. You've spent a lot of time on it, and we're very grateful.

"We were pretty much a pen and paper operating system, and with our growth, what we needed was to be able to look at the big picture and see exactly what we had: orders pending, orders completed, and it was getting really tough because of our growth. That involved everybody having a set time every day to coordinate, and just because of how busy we were getting, it became harder and harder, and this really solves those problems. Just that one screen showing all the pending jobs eliminated a lot of time.

"I came to you with a really simple idea: we wanted a work order that we could see on a computer. You basically took that idea and expanded on it. It's a real powerful tool that we don't know how to use yet. It's almost too easy to use. I mean, I'm real happy with it. There's not a lot of training. Eventually, it's going to free up so much time that we really don't know what the implications are at this point in time."

WHERE WE'VE BEEN, WHERE WE ARE

It's nice to think about how that all came about. You started with the business. Then—and, you'll admit, with a good bit of help—you

1. Collected planning statements and built formal Business Statements for the project area.
2. Identified the entities that represent the information used and collected in that area.
3. Defined the associations between the entities.
4. Defined the attributes that identify and describe information items.
5. Developed a data map.
6. All along the way, identified and corrected errors in the logical data model.
7. Applied the rules of business normalization to the data model.

Quite a job. But once you'd gone through all those steps, and done a lot of revision, you worked with the IT people to implement the data model as a database on an appropriate hardware and software platform.

Then there was building—good people, those—and testing and implementation. It was, you've got to admit, an educational experience, and not just an education in IT project management. Without everything you learned about the enterprise and its operations, and the decisions you (and the boss) made about how things should be done differently in the future ... well, you might still have become General Manager, but would you be able to do the job?

Not to worry. Nothing's perfect. The system will have to be tuned. The job's no piece of cake, especially with all the changes to the business. But that's the fun of it.

THE AUTHORS RESPOND

Our friend has achieved, albeit on a very small scale, Finkelstein's goal: to integrate "corporate strategic planning with systems development and data base design, so that the resulting strategic information systems provide direct support to management for decision-making" (1992: 3).

The process we've recommended is a logical and practical one, and it produces a logical data model that is in Third normal form. The logical data model is what gets turned over to the Database Administrator and the developers: it's the backbone of the system. From this point, we suggest using clustering (Finkelstein 1992: 424-437; Reingruber and Gregory 1994: 41-44). On that basis, the architect can identify units of work, the estimator can build the Gantt chart, and the project manager can assign development tasks to individuals.

With completion of the logical data model, the project isn't over, but it's well begun. That means it's half done.

References

Alexander, C., et al. 1977. *A Pattern Language*. New York, Oxford University Press.

Alpert, S. and K. Brown. 1998. *The Design Patterns Smalltalk Companion.* Reading, Massachusetts, Addison-Wesley.

Baklarz, G., et al. 2000. *DB2 Universal Database v7.1 for UNIX, Linux, Windows and OS/2 Database Administration Certification Guide.* 4th ed. Englewood Cliffs, NJ: Prentice Hall.

Barker, R. 1990. *CASE*Method: Entity Relationship Modelling.* Wokingham, England: Addison-Wesley.

Booch, G., et al. 1999. *The Unified Software Language User Guide.* Reading, Massachusetts: Addison-Wesley.

Burch, J., and G. Grudnitski. 1989. *Information Systems: Theory and Practice.* 5th ed. New York: Wiley.

Burek, P. 2004. CASE*Method: Entity Relationship Modeling: Barker's ERD notation and ist [sic] ontological extensions. Seminar presentation, "Prinzipien des Ontological Engineering." *Onto-Med*, http://www.onto-med.de/de/lehre/ws2003-04-ont-eng/VCase.ppt

Chamberlin, D. 1998. *A Complete Guide to DB2 Universal Database.* San Francisco: Morgan Kaufmann.

Chen, P. 1976. The Entity-Relationship Model - Toward a Unified View of Data. *ACM Trans. Database Syst.* 1(1): 9-36.
http://www.informatik.uni-trier.de/~ley/db/journals/tods/tods1.html#Chen76

Evitts, P. 2000. *A UML Pattern Language.* New York: Macmillan-Que.

Finkelstein, C. 1990. *An Introduction to Information Engineering: From Strategic Planning to Information Systems.* Sydney: Addison-Wesley.

Finkelstein, C. 1992. *Information Engineering: Strategic Systems Development.* Sydney: Addison-Wesley.

Finkelstein, C., and P. Aiken. 2000. *Building Corporate Portals with XML.* New York: McGraw-Hill.

Gamma, E., et al. 1995. *Design Patterns: Elements of Reusable Object-Oriented Software.* Reading, Massachusetts, Addison-Wesley.

Halpin, T. 2000. An ORM Metamodel of Barker ER. *Journal of Conceptual Modeling,* No. 17, Dec 2000. http://www.inconcept.com/JCM/December2000/halpin.html

IBM, iSeries Information Center. "Referential Integrity." http://publib.boulder.ibm.com/ html/as400/v4r5/ic2924/index.htm?info/db2/rbafymst136.htm

IBM, DB2 Technical Support. "SQL Reference: Constraints." www-306.ibm.com/cgi-bin/db2www/data/db2/udb/winos2unix/support/document.d2w/ report?fn=db2s0cnstrnt.htm

Kroenke, D. 2002. *Database Processing.* 8th ed. Englewood Cliffs, NJ: Prentice Hall. http://myphliputil.pearsoncmg.com/ student/ph_kroenke_databaseprocessing_8/ch04.ppt

Mullins, C. 2002. *Database Administration: The Complete Guide to Practices and Procedures.* Boston: Addison-Wesley.

Object Management Group. 2003. *Unified Modeling Language (UML), Version 1.5.* Specification, 1 March 2003. http://www.omg.org/docs/formal/03-03-01.pdf

Pree, W., and E. Gamma. 1995. *Design Patterns for Object-Oriented Software Development.* Reading, Massachusetts, Addison-Wesley.

Reingruber, M., and W. Gregory. 1994. *The Data Modeling Handbook.* New York: Wiley.

Rob, P., and E. Semaan. 2004. *Databases: Design, Development, and Deployment Using Microsoft Access.* 2nd ed. New York: Irwin McGraw-Hill.

Silverston, L., et al. 2001. *The Data Model Resource Book.* 2nd ed., 2 vols. New York: Wiley.

Standish Group. 1994. *The Chaos Report.* http://www.pm2go.com/sample_research/chaos_1994_1.php

U.S. Government. National Institute for Standards and Technology. Information Technology Laboratory. *Integration Definition for Information Modeling (IDEFIX) -- 93 Dec 21. Federal Information Processing Standards.* Publication 184: 1993 December 21. www.itl.nist.gov/fipspubs/by-num.

Visible Systems Corporation. Visible Advantage. www.visible.com.

Yourdon, E. 1989. *Modern Structured Analysis.* Englewood Cliffs, NJ: Yourdon Press.

Index

abbreviation, 124

acronym, 124, 156

Adobe Illustrator, 53

Adobe PDF, 121

alias, 111

association, viii, 22, 23, 24, 35, 38, 39, 40, 43, 46, 47, 48, 49, 50, 51, 52, 53, 63, 66, 67, 68, 69, 70, 75, 76, 78, 80, 81, 84, 85, 87, 89, 90, 91, 93, 94, 95, 97, 107, 129, 130, 131, 134, 136, 137, 138, 139, 140, 141, 142, 143, 147, 148, 161, 162, 170, 171, 172, 175, 176, 177, 178, 180, 184, 185, 188, 189, 191, 192, 199, 200, 201, 202, 203, 207, 213, 218

association line, 38, 39, 40

assumption, 8, 15

atomic attribute, 111, 112

attribute, viii, 18, 21, 35, 37, 46, 56, 57, 64, 65, 66, 67, 70, 73, 79, 84, 99, 102, 103, 107, 109, 110, 111, 112, 113, 114, 115, 116, 117, 118, 121, 122, 123, 124, 125, 129, 133, 138, 140, 150, 151, 152, 153, 157, 158, 159, 160, 163, 164, 169, 170, 173, 175, 180, 181, 184, 185, 187, 188, 191, 192, 198, 207, 209, 218

autonumber, 148

binary object, 121, 148

Boyce/Codd normal form (BCNF), 164

business event, 12, 17, 18, 23

business normalization, 5, 218

business process re-engineering, 12

business rule, viii, 12, 13, 17, 18, 22, 23, 32, 34, 37, 55, 72, 75, 99, 102, 127, 129, 161

Business Statement, viii, 5, 21, 22, 23, 28, 29, 30, 32, 34, 35, 37, 42, 43, 47, 58, 59, 60, 72, 86, 88, 90, 94, 101, 123, 127, 129, 137, 138, 139, 143, 144, 145, 158, 159, 167, 199, 218

candidate key, 124, 157, 164, 208

cardinality, 35, 40, 58, 60, 63, 85, 136, 198

categorizing association, 71, 180, 188, 191, 192

category, 21, 73, 77, 81, 93, 157, 180, 184, 185, 187, 188, 191, 192, 193